the song of roland

the song of roland

Translated, with an Introduction,

by

FREDERICK GOLDIN

W · W · NORTON & COMPANY

New York · London

Printed in the United States of America.

ALL RIGHTS RESERVED

W. W. Norton & Company, Inc., 500 Fifth Avenue, New York, N.Y. 10110

W. W. Norton & Company Ltd., 37 Great Russell Street, London WC1B 3NU

Library of Congress Cataloging in Publication Data
Chanson de Roland.   English.
  The song of Roland.
  Bibliography: p. 43
  1.   Roland—Romances.   I.   Goldin, Frederick.
PQ1521.E5G6   841'.1   78–16256

ISBN 0-393-09008-6

1 2 3 4 5 6 7 8 9 0

To Dione

Contents

Acknowledgments   *ix*

Synopsis   *1*

Introduction   *3*

    On Meter and Style   *28*

    Bibliography and Notes   *43*

A Note on the Translation   *47*

The Song of Roland   *51*

Acknowledgments

I want to thank the following people, who helped me and en-
couraged me and made things pleasant for me, at different times and
in various ways, during the many years (almost *set anz tuz pleins*) in
which I worked on this book:

Professor Hella Somogyi and Christina Haber, of Vienna;

Maurice and Norah O'Sullivan, of John Street, Dingle, County
Kerry;

Rosario Rodriguez and Luis Perez of New York City.

I also want to thank the Oesterreichische Nationalbibliothek and
the Universitätsbibliothek in Vienna for their courtesy and hospital-
ity.

I am grateful to John Francis, my editor at Norton, and to Nor-
man MacAfee, who copyedited the manuscript. They got rid of
many infelicities and suggested many changes for the better.

Whenever I withdrew to work on this book, it was always hearten-
ing to know that I would find four great champions when I emerged:
my children—Cheryl, Lisa, and Paul; and my wife, Dione, who has
helped in more ways than I can recount.

Finally, I want to acknowledge my debt to The City College of the
City University of New York, and especially the Department of En-
glish. It was there, as a student, that I started on the path that I have
followed ever since; and to this very day, when I write, I am guided
by the voices of two of the most inspiring teachers I have ever known:
Theodore Goodman, and Nathan Berall. Today I count myself for-
tunate to be a member of the faculty there, and in all my efforts I am
encouraged by the scholarship, the sense of community, and the
dedication of my colleagues in the Department of English.

The Song of Roland:

. . . begins with a trick the Saracens decide to play on Charlemagne. He has been warring in their land for seven long years, he has taken their citadels, killed or converted nearly all of their people. Now they have only one city left, Saragossa, and that appears doomed to fall.

The pagan king, Marsilion, in council with his wisest men, decides to send an embassy to Charlemagne entreating him to return to Aix, his capital, and promising to follow him there and become a Christian. That is the pagans' desperate trick: they have no intention of following him; but they can think of no other way to rid Spain of these Christian warriors. When the pagan embassy presents this proposal to Charlemagne and his barons, only one man—Roland—speaks against it. The others are weary of fighting and eager to return home. They see great merit in Marsilion's offer of peace. This is "the council that went wrong."

And now, whom will they send to carry their decision to Marsilion? It is a dangerous mission, for earlier, on a similar occasion, two of Charlemagne's noble vassals came to him bearing the same message, and Marsilion took their heads. And now again here are Charlemagne's brave vassals ready to make the journey to Saragossa. Naimon volunteers to go, and Roland, and Oliver, and Archbishop Turpin. Charlemagne refuses each in turn: he will not part with them. Then Roland names his stepfather, Ganelon; the barons immediately approve this choice. And Ganelon is furious. He is Roland's kinsman, yet Roland and his companions have put him in danger. Before the King and all his barons, he defies Roland, and Oliver, and the Twelve Peers.

And he does not have to wait long for the opportunity to get his revenge. Riding to Saragossa with the Saracen ambassador, Blancandrin, he explains how Christians and pagans can achieve lasting peace: kill the war party—Roland, Oliver, and the Twelve Peers—and there will be no more war. In Saragossa he shows Marsilion and his court how to bring about the death of these great vassals. They will be left in the rear-guard—Ganelon will make sure of that—when Charlemagne returns to France: ambush them. The conspiracy is sworn.

And so Ganelon returns to the Christian camp with good news: Marsilion, he says, has agreed to the Emperor's demands. Now it is time for the French army to withdraw. Whom shall they name to command the rear-guard? "Roland, my stepson," says Ganelon. And Roland proudly accepts that post, as Ganelon knew he would. The army returns in a long, winding column, stretched out through the defiles of the Pyrenees, and the rear-guard is left behind in Rencesvals.

When the army of the Franks is gone, the Saracens attack. The battle is long, and bitter. Oliver, Turpin, the Twelve Peers, and the 20,000 warriors of the rear-guard are killed. In the end only one man is left on the battlefield: Roland, dying. No man has killed him, but his temples have burst from the strain of sounding the ivory horn, the olifant, to call back the main army.

Charlemagne returns and annihilates Marsilion's host. But there is another great battle that he must fight. A huge army is on its way, led by Baligant, the supreme pagan lord. They rise up before Charlemagne just as he has buried the dead of Rencesvals and turned toward France. The terrible battle ends in single combat between the ancient lords of Christendom and heathendom.

The Emperor returns to Aix. Now it is time for the trial of Ganelon. In their speeches to the court, Charlemagne and Ganelon are in perfect agreement regarding the facts: Ganelon does not deny what he did. But he denies that it was treason. It was, he says, *revenge*, legally sanctioned and properly executed; he cannot, therefore, be condemned. Now what shall Ganelon's act be called? Shall it be called treason (in which case he must be executed) or revenge (in which case he must be set free)? The barons are unwilling to give it a name. The answer must come from God.

Introduction

In the year 777 the Saracen governor of Barcelona and Gerona, Sulaiman ibn Yaqzan ibn Al-Arabi, appeared before Charles, King of the Franks, to persuade him to bring his army into Spain. Al-Arabi had revolted against the authority of the Emir Abd al Rahman of Cordova (a rebel himself against the Abbassid caliphs), and he now made the following offer: if Charles came to his aid against the Emir, then Al-Arabi and his allies (among whom was the governor of Saragossa) would submit to the authority of the Franks. This meeting took place in Paderborn. Charles agreed.

The King led a column of his army into Spain in 778, took Pamplona, and arrived at Saragossa, where, according to plan, he was joined by a second column approaching from the east. From that moment on, things went wrong. Al-Arabi's supposed ally, the governor of Saragossa, kept the gates of the city closed and repudiated the agreement made in Paderborn. Charles besieged the city. For a month and a half the Frankish army lay beneath the walls of Saragossa. Then, at the end of July, Charles decided to give it up and return to France.

On the 15th of August, in the year 778, Charles's army was stretched out along the narrow defiles of the Pyrenees, bound for home. What happened on that day is told in a biography of Charles written some fifty years later, the *Vita Karoli* by Eginhard:[1]

> . . . on their journey home in that same pass through the Pyrenees, they had to suffer for a moment the treachery of the Basques [*Wasconicam perfidiam*]. It happened this way: as the army was proceeding, stretched out in a long thin column because of the narrowness of that defile, the Basques [*Wascones*] lay in ambush on top of a mountain—the place is thickly covered with woods and therefore well suited for such covert attacks; and they rushed down upon the end of the baggage train and upon those troops in the rear-guard who were protecting the main army ahead, forced them down to the bottom of the valley, engaged them in battle and killed them to the last man; then they looted the baggage, and protected by the gathering night they scattered in every direction with all the speed they had. In what took place the Basques were favored by the lightness of their arms and the terrain in which they fought; and the Franks were put thoroughly at a disadvantage by

3

the great weight of their arms and the unevenness of the ground.
In this battle were killed Eggihardus, seneschal of the royal table;
Anshelmus, count of the palace; and Hruodlandus, prefect of the
marches of Brittany, among many others.

This disaster is the historic kernel of *The Song of Roland*. The
presence of the Frankish army in Spain, as well as one can judge
from shreds of evidence pieced together from many sources, both
Carolingian and Saracen, seems to have been the result of a power
play by the great King, who apparently saw in the internal strife of
the Spanish Saracens a chance to extend his realm. It ended badly
for everyone (except the *Wascones*), and it was a bitter memory to the
King for the rest of his life, judging from the fact that the full scope of
the disaster—the destruction of the rear-guard and the plundering of
the baggage train—was not disclosed in any Carolingian document
until after Charles was dead. No crusading intent can be detected in
this enterprise, though there were attempts both before the event (in
the benediction of Pope Hadrian upon the departure of the army)
and especially afterward, to give it such a coloring, as though
Charles had entered Spain to protect the Christians from the cruel
yoke of Saracen oppression—an oppression that in fact did not exist.[2]
This is the poor, bare, inglorious event, a thwarted enterprise end-
ing in a painful loss. Between this sad date of August 15, 778, and
the composition—probably between 1095 and 1100—of the poem
we now possess in the Oxford manuscript,* there is an interval of
some 300 years. The poem before us now has retained little of the
historic event apart from the last name mentioned among the fallen
and the annihilation of the rear-guard on the homeward march
through the Pyrenees. Somehow this non-event has been enlarged
into a great epic of treachery and loyalty, and this humiliating defeat
at the hands of unknown brigands transformed into a holy crusade, a
glorious martyrdom, a great apocalyptic victory ordained by God.
It is no wonder that nearly everyone who has studied this poem
since the manuscript was rediscovered and then published in 1837
has been fascinated by the question of its origin. How did those
unedifying events of 777–78 lead to the creation of *The Song of
Roland*? Was it the work of a single poet or of generations of poets?
Was it created all at once or by continual accretion over a long
period? This much is certain: there are documents that show that

---

* The Oxford manuscript (Digby 23 in the Bodleian) is the oldest known extant ver-
sion of *The Song of Roland*, written between 1125 and 1150 in Anglo-Norman French.
Since the manuscript is a copy at least once removed from the archetype, its
dialect tells us little about the French of the original. For a study of the entire manu-
script tradition, see Cesare Segre, *La Tradizione della 'Chanson de Roland'* (Milan
and Naples, 1974).

before the composition of the Oxford *Roland*, during those three centuries, there developed an oral tradition centered on the battle at Rencesvals.[3] "Someone invented the Emir Baligant, as someone invented Turpin's participation in the battle, as someone invented Oliver, as someone invented Ganelon, as someone invented the beautiful Aude."[4] Whoever put the Oxford *Roland* together might have invented Baligant, but he inherited all of the other important characters and events in the story, for they were famous before he did his work. Who he was, however, and how he worked, and what he had to work with, are all matters of dispute.

Whatever the circumstances in which it was composed, *The Song of Roland* looks back: it tells a tale that is set in the past. By the time of the Oxford version it was the remote and therefore the glorious and exemplary past, a golden age in the age of grace. It was looked upon as the time when the great dream of Christendom had come true, when a worldwide Christian community was established under a pious and crusading Emperor, and all men were bound in ascending loyalty to each other and to the Lord of all. The Carolingian Empire was seen as the fulfillment of a divine intention.

The numerous "errors" in this representation and in the figure and career of Charlemagne are frequently pointed out and sometimes rashly attributed to the poet's (or poets') ignorance. Charlemagne was in fact thirty-seven and not yet Emperor when the rearguard was ambushed: he was the King of the Franks, and he was not 200 years old; he wore a mustache but never a beard (which became à la mode in the eleventh century). Islam is and was monotheistic and forbade graven images of God: no Saracen ever prayed to the idols of that motley trio Mahum, Apollin, and Tervagant. The poet's many "errors" in geography have also been duly noted—Saragossa lies in the valley of the Ebro and not on a high mountain; and all those unidentifiable place names—though often at the cost of obscuring his poetic truth: for the fantastic name of every place locates it unerringly in the realm of God's enemies or in the sweet land of His servants. If one reads the poem as a chronicle, one can compile a tremendous list of such errors. But that is not how the poem should be read. The poet himself calls upon a chronicle, the *Geste Francor*, at certain times, usually to support what looks like a verifiable statement of fact, and in referring to such a chronicle he explicitly distinguishes his own narrative from one.

Judged rightly, these are not errors at all but essential elements in the picture that the poem presents. The great value one derives from studying the facts and identifying the "errors" is that one learns what has been rejected as unfit for the representation set forth in *The Song of Roland*. As it happens, nearly every detail of the historical incident has been rejected: history knew only a terrible defeat; the song reveals a glorious victory. But if Saragossa, that last pagan citadel, had really been set upon a towering eminence, or if Charles had really been 200 years old and at all similar to that patriarchal figure with the great beard white as the flowers of April, it is safe to say that the poem would have preserved, with lingering accuracy, these revealing historical facts; and we can be sure that the victory over Baligant would never have been invented if anything like it had ever occurred. For the poem sets forth the vision of an exemplary past—the past *as it had to be,* given the way things are; the past that guides the present and enjoins the future.

We see in the Charlemagne of the epic, not the historical king and emperor, but the true and accurate representation of an ideal ardently praised at the time the poem was cast into its present form, around the year 1100.[5] Today we read a poem created in the distant past in which the poet looks back to a past even more remote, holding out to his audience the picture of an age when things were as they ought to be and all men were in their right places—an inspiring age that must be brought to earth again, when all Christian powers oriented themselves in homage to this great man, wise with the wisdom of 200 years of God's grace.

The positive historical context in which this vision of the past arose is usually identified as the long struggle of the Capetian rulers to centralize political power in France.[6] From the death of Charlemagne in 814, the Carolingian kings presided over less and less, apart from the expanding dissolution of the empire; their lands and their powers were lost to the great barons, and in the end the king was a mere figurehead whose realm barely extended beyond Paris. Then, in 987, the last Carolingian king was gone, and a new line was established by Hugh Capet. From that moment on, he and all his descendants—including Philip I (1060–1108), who reigned when the Oxford *Roland* was composed—were involved in the struggle to bring the barons under the king's power. *The Song of Roland* is often held to be a kind of propaganda, a defense and glorification of royal power—the principle of the supreme sovereignty of the king is explicitly introduced into the poem in the trial of Ganelon, and it is authenticated in the judicial battle of Tierri and Pinabel, in which the judgment of God is revealed.

It is therefore a mistake to look in this poem for an account of the life of a particular period, whether in the eighth or the eleventh century: that approach leads to the preoccupation with "errors." The poem shows us something else, something that a work of literature can show better than any chronicle or history: we see how an age regarded its past, recreated history in order to find precedence and dignity for its own aspirations. It may be true that the early Capetian rulers wanted some historical sanction to strengthen the poor foundations of their rule and commanded this version of the poem so that the glory of Charlemagne would shine on them. Whatever practical intention there may have been, the poem transcends it. *The Song of Roland* speaks to any age that wants to see its present struggles as something more than the madness of accidents and lusts, as something noble and necessary, as an ordained part of a vast integrity. There is a great difference, however, between the way in which we regard the past that engendered us and the way the poem looks to the past in which its action is set. The past it revealed to its earliest audiences was really a vision of their future.[7] Those who shared that past were to give their support to the King's great struggle, a struggle that aimed not to *progress* from that auspicious time when angels came down from heaven and the sun stood still to help the Emperor defend all Christendom, but to *return* to it, to regain what had been lost: a perfect state pleasing to God.

Once this line into the past is begun, it can be extended infinitely further back. When Charlemagne, Roland, and Turpin pray, they look back to those who lived in an even earlier time but still command a vivid presence. Daniel in the lion's den, the three Hebrew children in the fiery furnace, Jonah in the belly of the great fish: these are not only the ones who came first, they are also brother heirs to Roland and Charlemagne and Turpin, sharers in God's loyalty and love, less separated by time from those who recall them in prayer than joined to them as fellow servants of the one Lord who protects them.

Therefore, in the figure of Charlemagne, religious and political aspirations are united; he is at the center of history's pattern, the nexus between the past and the future. For the same line that connects this old poem to an even older time, and to the beginning of time, can be extended into the future as well, to the end of time, when the empire of Charlemagne is upon the earth again. Those last days are foreshadowed by the action in the poem. For near the end of time, as God's word in Revelation foretells, the Antichrist will come who will suborn the human race when it is on the verge of sanctity, and he will rule until he is defeated by the angelic hordes of heaven—a battle prefigured in the song by the Baligant episode, whose apocalyptic imagery, as has long been recognized, shows the full range of the poet's vision.[8]

The poem's frame of reference, therefore, is infinite, ranging from before the beginning to after the end of time. And once we see the vastness of that frame, we can see how much is left out of it: *we* are left out, or at least everything personal and unique about us, the selves we know. For the vision of the poem is blind to our own linear notion of time: it cannot see that values change, it cannot conceive that one day human beings may stand in a different relation to those who rule and even to the Lord of all—to that Lord whose immanent justice and, in fact, whose very existence, they may, with perfect integrity, deny. In its apocalyptic vision and in its blindness to the conditions in which we make our way, it demands that we join in the struggle to bring back again the state and the age over which Charlemagne ruled. For it says in its very first line and repeatedly thereafter: *nostre emperere!* "Our Emperor!" We do not have to answer the poem's demand in order to read it aright. But we do have to see that it makes a demand, that the tale it tells contains an injunction upon the audience, that its vision surpasses the frame of its narrative.

When the poem looks to the future, then, it does not see us—at least not in the skins that we inhabit. It sees a pattern that involves all of the generations of mankind: the drama of redemption, foreseen by God. It is by the authority of that pattern that the poem enlists all of its audiences into the struggle to restore the state that God has blessed. We do not share that vision, and yet, because the language and style of the poem assume the immediate and corroborating presence of an audience—*our Emperor!*—even we, at this great distance, have a certain role to play. We are cast into that role by a world-view that is as deep and complicated regarding time as it is narrow and indifferent regarding space. This sense of organic time—time that stretches in a providential pattern over all creatures past, present, and future, and makes them contemporaries—puts us within the moral grasp of the poem and into its very action, no matter who we are and no matter how thoroughly we reject its feudal notions of faith and authority. For though we may reject that pattern as historical truth, we can still feel its effect as a poetic strategy, a way of calling upon the audience to complete the meaning of the song, and of heightening our awareness of the poet's conception of time and of the poem's origin in history. "Let no bad songs be sung about us," says Roland, meaning: let songs be sung in our praise—and that means: *this* song, the Oxford *Roland*, witnessed by this audience—by us.[9] The song's enduring ability to win an audience is just what Roland wished for, the fulfillment of all his boasts and promises, like his triumphant death. We today still witness the story of a brave man keeping faith, even though his faith is not ours, and our notion of bravery is, thank God, far different from his. For the song, by assuming our presence, puts us into the position of witnesses. We are, with all our disbelief, maneuvered by the providential strategy of the poem. As we read, we become that laudatory future *now,* and our attendance on the song is Roland's continual victory. We will most probably come away from this dialogue across the ages with all our disbelief intact; but as soon as we see how the song positions us, we can also see how the song presents itself, how it wants its narrative to be read, or heard: as a vision of history stretching across time and encompassing us, as revelation.

The Song of Roland is a *chanson de geste*, an Old French epic poem about the exploits (Latin *gesta*) of a great vassal in the service of his lord (or, as in certain later poems, in revolt against his lord). The lord that Roland serves is depicted as the Emperor of Christendom; Charlemagne, in turn, is in the service of the supreme Lord of heaven, and so the feudal pyramid rises above the world to end in the Author of all existence. The close relation between the epic genre of this poem, the feudal society it depicts, and the religious war that comprises nearly all of its action is the principle of its unity, and many errors of interpretation occur when one forgets what holds the poem together.

Paien unt tort e chrestïens unt dreit, says Roland, rallying his men (line 1015); *Nos avum dreit, mais cist glutun unt tort*, he says again, in the midst of the battle: pagans are wrong and Christians are right; we are right and these swine are wrong. Nowadays, of course, nobody has the right to talk like that, and so this famous exhortation is often condemned as a soldier's mindless partisanship. But in fact Roland is stating a major theme of the poem: the life of the feudal vassal can have no value unless it is sanctified by service to God. The pagan vassals are exact doubles of Christian vassals—they are brave, meticulously hierarchized, faithful to their lords; they wear the same armor, they have their councils, their battle-cries, their twelve peers, their famous swords, and their men of wisdom—and so the one radical difference between the two sides in this poem is exactly what Roland says it is, the fact that Christans are right and pagans are wrong.[10] The pagans have devoted all of their virtues and their vast feudality to the worship of false gods; and so the greater their nobility, the greater their crimes and treasons. The pagans are loyal, but their loyalty is obstinacy, because they are against God and steadfast in their refusal to worship Him. The Christians are savage in battle, but their savagery is sanctified, transformed into the zeal of martyrdom, because they are justified by God. The poet goes to great pains to show how the Saracen structure reflects the Christian at every point; it is because they are the enemies of God and worship Mahumet that the pagans can never be more than reflections. Roland's famous utterance therefore means exactly the opposite of what it is often taken to mean. It is the warrior's expression of humility, his understanding that without the belief in God we are all *glutun*. Roland is a Christian vassal and knows that without the grace of God his great qualities would lead him to perdition.

One must always be mindful of the Christian inspiration of *The Song of Roland*. The immanent justice of God is the ground upon which the entire poem is constructed.[11] Every formal conflict in the poem is defined as a judicial battle whose outcome is God's verdict for the victor and against the vanquished. The pagans vastly outnumber the 20,000 Christians of the rear-guard; Baligant's hordes swarm over the countryside, far superior in size to Charles's army (ten divisions versus three times ten); the physically mediocre Tierri is by any normal standard no match for the great fighter Pinabel, whose towering presence intimidates all the barons of Charlemagne's empire—except for this one unremarkable man. In each case the miraculous victory of the smaller side reveals the will of God, for only He could have caused the astonishing outcome. Whatever propagandizing purpose it may have been meant to serve, the Oxford *Roland* is a religious poem because every event in it (including the establishment of the King's supremacy) is finally revealed as ordained by God, though there may be a secular precedent that looks like a cause; because all of its ethical values, though they are expressed in feudal terms, are ultimately justified as forms of Christian virtues; because all of its battles are cast as questions addressed to Him, and all of its victories are cast as His answer.

The ultimate religious reference of the poem clarifies its genre as well. To see this, we have to consider the kind of questions that the epic, especially the *chanson de geste*, is meant to answer. Many readers of *The Song of Roland*, for example, are distressed when they try to account for the motives behind certain actions, or to judge their moral value. What lies behind the hostility of Roland and Ganelon? Why does Ganelon explode with such murderous rage when he is named to carry out a plan that he himself had argued for? Why does he threaten Roland before the Emperor confirms the barons' choice? Above all, why does Ganelon commit treason? Or: Roland refuses to sound the olifant and thus ensures the martyrdom of the rear-guard. *Should* he have refused, many ask; was he right, or was he the victim of *démesure*, a term used by many who have written on this poem (but never by the one who composed it) to designate recklessness and inordinate pride?[12] Does he regret the deaths he might have prevented; does he repent before he dies? And soon we find ourselves plagued by questions that arise from the moral uncertainty of everyday life—but not from the poem.

For the poem tells a story purportedly based on history—and in history, too, motives are often obscure and usually held to be less important than events. Furthermore, though the poem is not unconcerned with human motives, it does not—cannot—recognize the values upon which our judgments of our contemporaries are based; and the rash condemnation of Roland's act often expresses nothing more than what we all would think of a man who did the same thing today. Questions such as whether Roland should have acted as he did are out of court. They address themselves to a false issue and raise doubts concerning values regarded in the work itself as beyond questioning; they are alien to the epic world, obscurantist, and anachronistic, for the alternatives implied in such questions belong to another time and to another genre, with another truth to tell. That other genre, in the medieval period, is the romance, a courtly form adapted to the depiction of individual moral experience. Some of the differences between these two kinds of narrative are spelled out in the following passage:[13]

> The *chanson* [*de geste*] presents a coherent relation between one event and another, the romance a series of episodes that are, as far as their content is concerned, completely independent of one another. For the *chanson*, therefore, the surface development of the action is far more important than it is for the romance. . . . In the beginning there is an event that sets the action in motion; the action then runs its course almost on its own, autonomously, and the poem closes at that point where the chain of events (which began with that initial action) comes to an end. Every single episode has its fixed place in the totality of the action; it cannot be arbitrarily omitted or moved to another place without disturbing the progress of the narrative. The aesthetic unity that develops in this way is first of all a unity of the surface: it lies in the coherence and self-containment of the sequence of events. . . .
>
> In the romance, on the other hand, each episode appears to be governed by coincidence and arbitrariness. . . . Its aesthetic unity is to be grasped not in the surface action but in the agent, the hero.
>
> In the *chanson*, too, the hero can play a dominant rôle, but he is always in the service of the action, as its agent. One can see this most clearly in the fact that the hero can change in the course of the poem. In the *Chanson de Roland*, for example, the action does not end with Roland's death: from the point of view of the whole work, the most crucial part has not yet even come. After Roland, Charles takes over the action and leads it to a conclusion. This changing of the agent is not felt as a break, because the unity of the *chanson* lies not in the person of the hero but in the encompassing continuity of the action.

The motives of the epic hero are therefore determined by the action. They conform to a well-known course of events, which the audience is willing to accept as historical fact. The story related in an epic is always a version of some famous and significant historical event, some episode that is crucial, or held to be crucial, in the history of the people among whom the epic arises. Epic action thus has an historical core: it is centered on a past event. Even if the story is fictitious, the events in it are treated as though they had really occurred in the past and engendered the present state of things. For the epic is concerned with "actions irremediably completed."[14]

Since the epic must have an historical core, it must always look back, and its point of view will always be anchored in the presence of its audience. Both the poet and the audience look back to a critical moment in history, the event from which their world emerged, the past they share in every performance. For the epic genre is rooted in the idea of performance; every epic poem needs listeners in attendance. Even if those listeners are utterly alien in time and place, they are bound to the poem. For if the pastness of epic action is essential, there must be a present audience—even if it is an implicit audience—by which that pastness is established and the continuance of its effect realized. Nowadays the old epic poem has an audience of readers, and we look back to other moments in the past to find the roots of our being. But the poem will not modify its demand on us; it insists with even greater conviction: *Charlemagne is our Emperor.* And so the poem's effect on us depends on our willingness to respond to its words, at least for the time that we play the role of audience, as though we were not alien to this remote part of the human past. For, in fact, this moment too is at the root of our being.

In this one respect we today can identify ourselves with those who heard this poem in the beginning, because we take up a similar position regarding the time in which the action is set. We corroborate its retrospective point of view, we complete its context: with every performance, or with every reading, the presence of the audience establishes the pastness of the action. The audience therefore plays an indispensable role in the creation of the epic world: it calls that world forth by looking back upon it. Now there is a famous passage in Boethius that analyzes what takes place when one regards an action in the past, and the terms he uses will be of great help to us. In Book Five the lady Philosophy speaks as follows:

And I will answer you by saying that a future event, when it is referred to God's omniscience, appears necessary; but when that same future event is considered in its own nature, it appears to be completely free and undetermined. For there are two kinds of necessity: one is simple, absolute—for example, it is by necessity that all human beings are mortal; the other exists only in a particular condition, so that *if you know* that someone is walking, he must necessarily be walking; for when something is known, it cannot be otherwise than as it is known. But this condition in no way involves the other kind of necessity, simple necessity; for what makes the thing that is known necessary is not its own nature but the condition that is added: no inherent necessity forces a man walking of his own free will to step forward; however, *if* he walks, he is necessarily stepping forward. In the same way, an event that Providence sees as occurring must necessarily be, even though it may have no necessity by its own nature. Now God sees the occurrence of future things that come forth from the freedom of the will, sees them as present things; and so these future things, if they are referred to God's vision of them, are made necessary by the fact that He knows they are to occur, by the condition of divine knowledge; but considered in themselves they do not relinquish the absolute freedom of their own natures. Without doubt, therefore, all those things will occur that God knows are going to occur. But some of these things happen as the result of free will; and these things, though they occur, do not by coming into existence lose their own nature, by which, before they occurred, they were able not to occur. (V, 6, 124–126)

The world of *The Song of Roland* is ruled by conditional necessity, *necessitas condicionis*. The condition that makes things necessary is "added," as Boethius says, to every event in that world, and it is we, the audience, who add it. Before we become an audience, we know, or are expected to know, what has occurred in history, or in the revered legend that the poem regards as the most authentic history; and so on becoming an audience we know what is going to happen in the tale we listen to: our ordinary knowledge becomes foreknowledge, becomes an analogy of divine providence, and every event in the epic is made necessary (in the Boethian sense) by the fact that we know it is going to occur, by the condition of the audience's knowledge. We know what happened in history; and since this or that event lies entirely in the past, we know further that it is a part of the history of the world thus far, that it participates in a transcendental design: it therefore has to happen, it is *necessary*.

Epic action is set in the past, as required by the genre. The historical event is now viewed within the frame of a narrative; it is integrated into a vast structure, endowed with significance, exempted from chance: the aesthetic form of the epic reflects the transcendental design of history. And since the epic event is thus completely enacted and framed, it is fully present to us in all its moments, we know it from beginning to end. Therefore, we can say, prompted by Philosophy: we know that we will walk, and therefore he *must* walk; for we knew, before the first notes of the song were intoned and we became an audience, that he *did* walk. We know—and our knowledge precedes every event, every cause, every motive—that Roland will refuse to sound the olifant: therefore, his refusal is necessary, for it is accomplished. The witnessed and believed authenticity of his act is all that counts. His motives, whatever they are, are at best secondary causes, completely determined by the action and significant in this poem, not because of what they bring about, but because of what they reveal: the loyal spirit of a true hero. We must regard his great spirit, his proud motives, and his famous act as praiseworthy, exemplary, pleasing to God, because they are necessary, foreseen, exactly as they occurred, in the destiny of Sweet France. For otherwise the *Geste Francor* would be nothing but the history of accidents and whims.

We have no right to ask: *should* he have done what he did? shouldn't he have considered another way? shouldn't he have been more reasonable? Questions like these deny the terribly necessity of history and the monumental dignity of the epic. They are questions brought in from the Age of the Team. Once we view the epic world from a true perspective, that of an audience witnessing the reenactment of an unalterable past, we see a world governed only by providential force. *Within* that world, however, considered only in his nature, the epic hero moves in his own present with undiminished freedom of the will: "I would be a fool to sound the olifant," says he; or "I shall strike a thousand seven hundred blows." The unpredictable present and the immutable past thus wonderfully coincide in an epic poem.

It is the past, or rather the audience's sense of the past, that ennobles these figures and their deeds, as it determines the form and technique of the poem. Because of the double perspective from which we, the audience, view the action—we see it looking back from our present, and looking forward from the hero's present—we experience at once in every figure and event the two forces of a free human will and a transcendental historic purpose. This is obviously true of an epic poem like *The Song of Roland*, in which this purpose is revealed as divine Providence: in Charlemagne's dreams,[15] for example, or in the three judicial battles, the will of God announces itself. But even when all the figures and events are the consequences of a mindless causality devoid of purpose, we still recognize the presence of a transcendent design. That is because every epic presents its narrative as history, no matter if it is really a fiction. It demands of us that we regard its action, down to the rightness of the last detail, as a crucial part of the real past—of the *living* past, for the world that surrounds us as we listen derives from it. Even if some event were in its inception completely accidental, it was nevertheless caused, and it produced consequences that led, in turn, to a ramifying pattern of causes; and so, what began as an accident becomes bound by causality and consequence to the ineradicable continuity of the past. For if we were to recreate the fabric of history, we would need this event to weave into our pattern. No matter how it happened, it has led somehow to the present state of things, to the facts we find in our world and the condition of our community, and so becomes, as we look back upon it, a part of the providential past: as things have turned out, it has served a purpose; therefore, it is necessary.

In case all this sounds too theoretical and abstract, let us consider two concrete examples. We can get some idea of how a thing is ennobled by our sense of its pastness if we consider how the death of someone we have loved or admired affects our feelings about his life. Sometimes death is a frightening specter, when it is almost in our ken: we get glimmerings of it, especially when we are ill. At such times we are frightened because we suddenly become aware that our body follows laws that pre-existed us and will go on after us, laws we never made or even properly understood; all of a sudden our body no longer belongs to us, it is no longer the agent of our will, it responds to something that eludes our knowledge. Its governance is now taken over by another reality, another life, something that seems utterly alien to us but awes us by its immensity, its absoluteness, its intimacy. And so it sometimes happens that when someone we love has died, we identify his personal reality with that larger reality that ruled his body, and we find ourselves thinking of his death as an incredible achievement, for we magnify his image with the greatness of that which engulfed him. Somehow, in dying, he has grown larger, become ancient and infinite; and our sense of that vast causality blots out our awareness of chance and circumstance—his whole life takes on the coherence and inevitability of the laws that ordained his extinction. Everything that was gratuitious and accidental in his life now becomes inevitable with his death. For no law decreed his existence: he did not have to live; but once he lived, he had to die. What had seemed to be the purposeless welter of his experience—the meaningless color of his eyes, the incoherence of his enthusiasms, the unpredictability of his indifferences, the chance occurrence of his neighborhoods, the wild inconsequence that followed his choices—now, in the light of his extinction, reveals an inspiring necessity. Now it can be seen that all his sleeping and waking moments were required exactly as they were to complete the form of his life. This is when we think of him in a few essential poses—working with the tools of his trade, sleeping on his side with his hand under his head, listening to the news on the radio; and our every image of him is the illustration of an epithet—he is the skilled, the childish, the gentle one, the unjudging, the long-sleeping, the incorruptible—for we see him now transfigured with significance, a reality defined for all eternity. The things about him that irritated us when he was alive, if we remember them at all, we think of now as derived from his essential meaning. We regard him now as a perfect being, an aesthetic triumph, the fulfillment of an idea—a father, a prophet, a fool, an irreplaceably ordinary man, but in any case unique, for his specific life and death were ordained.

What about the death of someone we neither love nor admire? Here we can find an example in American history, in an event whose centennial coincided with the bicentennial celebration of our origins.[16] Again we can see how conditional necessity transfigures men and events. In 1876 General George Armstrong Custer led the Seventh U.S. Cavalry, despite numerous warnings and apparently acting in disobedience of orders, into an ambush. He and his entire division were annihilated in the combined attack of the Sioux and Cheyenne, led by Sitting Bull and Crazy Horse. Since then historians and American history buffs have reexamined the various possibilities of the situation. Should he have attacked the numerically superior Indians? How would it all have turned out had he ordered the region to be properly reconnoitered, had he not been so hungry for fame, had he not desired a promotion so keenly, had he awaited (as he was supposed to) the arrival of the division led by his superior, had he not—like Roland—longed for a glorious victory?

We have a right, and perhaps even a duty, to ask such questions, because we know that this episode was completely unnecessary: the General could have acted otherwise. The massacre was gratuitous, the result of pure coincidence—it could have *not* occurred. For this event took place only because a fool on the one side and two brilliant strategists on the other found themselves in the same place at the same time.

And it is now more than a hundred years old, it is part of our past. One may claim, with some pride, that the passage of time has not conferred upon this event the dignity of necessity. And yet time and the sense of the past have in fact done their work. This event is permanently recorded in our history as an act of madness, the result of a single man's grotesque conviction and ambitiousness and a whole nation's crusading spirit and racist zeal; and it has, enlarged in this fashion, taken on something of the quality of the poet's marveling portraits of Ganelon. Even in raw history Custer's madness has achieved a classic ingloriousness, even a kind of satanic dignity, as a point of reference for the nation that went on to Vietnam, as the American *locus classicus* of moral imbecility and self-destruction.

But suppose this event were to be related in an epic. Then there would be another kind of transformation: all these accidents would immediately become inevitabilities. For the *condicio* would be added: lacking necessity in themselves, they would become necessary by being viewed from the perspective of a transcendent vision—providence and posterity know that these things will happen. We embarrassed and suspicious descendants would now become the audience, conscious both of the pastness of the event and of the epic form; and in that role we would, by our vision, transform the event into an enactment of necessity. Then the General's recklessness would become exemplary courage, an essential virtue of the American hero; the senseless slaughter would become a blessed martyrdom, the fulfillment of a sacred covenant; and above all, the defeat would become the first moment of an ordained rebirth. All these transformations would take place because our vision had enclosed the event in an historical and aesthetic frame that signifies that everything within is foreseen and therefore necessary. Looking back as inhabitants of the world that has emerged since then, we would see not an isolated catastrophe but the most critical moment in a providential structure. The question whether the General also acted as he did because he wanted a promotion would now be eradicated by the force of conditional necessity and replaced by motives better suited to the grand design.

Was the "real" Roland—the "original" uncrusading Hruodlandus, prefect of the Breton march, whose name appears, perhaps added by a later hand, in a few of the manuscripts of Eginhard's biography of Charlemagne—was this Roland, like Custer, a reckless fool, unmindful of the welfare of his men? Judging from all that we know of the original incident, Hruodlandus never had the choice that confronts the hero of the epic; he had no chance to summon help, much less to decide whether he should. All that we can surmise is that he fought bravely in a hopeless situation. We also surmise that nothing more specific was known about him during the genesis of the poem. Whatever the circumstances in which this poem came into being, there were no hard facts that could prevent those who sang the song from magnifying Hruodlandus into Roland.

But we know too much about Custer to make him an exemplary figure; there are too many witnesses to his nasty egotism and his lack of self-control. We cannot, without criminally deluding ourselves, give him the character of an epic hero, one that is worthy of receiving the commandments of necessity. Let us therefore give thanks that no one we know of has attempted anything of this sort, apart from a few foolish lyrics of the time and some "epic" movies since then. But simply from toying with this idea we can see that the hero's motives can never truly explain what takes place in the poem: they are mirrors, rather than movers, of epic action. For the hero would be diminished and his deeds trivialized if (like Custer) he had nothing but his own reasons and he were not appointed by history.

As epic necessity imposes coherence on the past, so it bestows dignity on men and events, for it removes them from the vanity of a personal will and identifies them with a divine intention. Necessity eradicates accidentality and creates, with its tremendous retrospective power, a need for every moment. The hero's motives are exactly right, even when he appears to a lesser man (like Oliver) to be most willful and undisciplined, for they realize a purpose too great for ordinary men to understand. He desires, with all his character and vitality, to bring about the crucial facts of history. Roland does what he does because he must do it, because the event has already taken place, in our view, and he has no choice. He is the agent of an accomplished action, and we are privileged to witness the true hero's graceful conformity to the rule of necessity.

Because we know the history of these events, we see Roland's acts as part of a pattern; and though we may later force ourselves to change our minds, we first see every pattern as the product of a deliberate will. For the point of view that sees, or projects, an immense design where there is only the welter of blind causality is a religious point of view; and so, even when we reject the substance of religion, we adopt its view of history when we are the audience of an epic poem. Roland's acts are part of an historical pattern, and we perceive them as emanating from the Will that produces history. Because of the ennobling effect of necessity, because his actions are always sanctioned by the demands of that transcendent pattern that we, in our present role as audience, cannot dissociate from the movement of a higher will, the hero can never be denounced as vain, or proud, or lacking in wisdom; nor, it follows, can his enemy ever be dismissed as simply a scoundrel. We must never judge Roland's motives by our common freedom and our common sense, because they are purely epic motives, his personal resolve to bring about what has already been enacted. Thus it is through necessity that the epic hero realizes his greatness and his humility; for he is the agent of providence.

The poet has exploited the effect of the pastness of the action and has arranged the narrative so as to put Roland's eminence beyond doubt; at the very least, if we do not simply admire Roland's actions, we refrain from judging them. But we are meant to admire them. Roland is the only one who knows the right thing to do when the Christians are confronted with Marsilion's offer of peace. The others have every conceivable good reason for accepting that offer. For one thing, nobody in the council knows that it is a trick. And Marsilion does promise to become Christian: his conversion was the object of Charlemagne's expedition. Naimon and Ganelon speak ably from principles—the highest principles. Roland speaks from experience—Basile and Basan had been slain earlier through Marsilion's treachery on a similar occasion: if Marsilion tricked them then, it is likely that he is tricking them now. They must not give up all that they have achieved for a mere promise; the war that Charlemagne came to fight is not over. But the others do not listen, for they are reasonable, and tired.

The scene in Charlemagne's court bears comparison with a scene in another medieval poem in which men make a choice in a necessitarian world, Chaucer's *Troilus and Criseyde.* The characters in that work are involved in a tremendous providential upheaval, the *translatio imperii*, the movement of the center of universal authority from Greece to Rome. Now for this great event to take place, Troy must be destroyed and Aeneas must make his escape; and for Troy to be destroyed, it must take in the agent of its destruction, the traitor Antenor. All of the characters are of course in the dark concerning the great moment in the history of salvation about to occur, and everything hinges on their reaction to the Greek offer to give them back their warrior Antenor in exchange for Criseyde. Hector sets before them the simplest and most obvious dictate of their moral code: their worth and dignity lie in their refusal to trade women. But the others think it would be mad to keep a useless woman when they can get a great warrior back. They are free to make their choice, and they choose the course that leads to their annihilation. Thus, as the matter is arranged by the poet, the freedom of the human will is preserved even as the force of necessity prevails; for though the Trojans did not know about the vast designs of Providence, they knew enough, especially after Hector had told them, to make the right decision, the one that would have excluded the traitor and saved the city.

The situation is worked out in the great English poem to reveal the moral failing of the Trojan populace; that same situation is developed to a different end in *The Song of Roland.* Like Hector, Roland tells the barons all that they need to know in order to make the right decision. We do not see in this any sign of a moral failing among the barons—they are all men of principle worn out with fighting—and least of all any sign of Roland's *démesure* or bellicosity. What takes place is the revelation of Roland's privileged position in the world. He is right, and all the others are wrong—and that is all: this scene does not show that he is right for the wrong reasons, or that Naimon is wrong for the right ones—two impossible and inconceivable ideas in the Middle Ages; it does not even show that his natural and unaided judgment is better than theirs. It simply shows that he is graced with the right decision. But in the world that this poem celebrates, he cannot be right by accident: not only his decision but his entire attitude is right—his militant response to the pagans, his whole sense of what a Christian knight must do is nearest to what pleases God, for it comes from God.

The massacre at Rencesvals does not begin with Roland's refusal to sound the olifant: it begins right here, in "the council that went wrong," as the poem says.[17] And we are expected to respond to Roland's act at Rencesvals in the light of the grace bestowed upon him in this council, remembering always that he is right, that the perilous position of the rear-guard would never have come about if his voice in council had carried the day, and that after Roland's death Charles ends up doing exactly what Roland had urged; so that the fact of his having been right then confers an authority upon his actions now, at Rencesvals. For judge him as one will, if he was bellicose, impulsive, proud, and foolish in council (that is how Ganelon judges him), he is all of those things now; and he was right then—these qualities led him, completely unaware of Marsilion's plan, to make the right decision. Now the pattern repeats itself at Rencesvals, and Naimon's wisdom is replaced by Oliver's wisdom. We the audience, knew that Roland was right in council because Marsilion's perfidy had been enacted before us. He is doing now what he did then, following the dictates of the Christian vassal's calling with unquestioning faith, though now we cannot see the corroborative light.

Still, it may be there, and the possibility of its presence, the inappropriateness of our moral categories to Roland's act, the very fact that what he does eludes definitive judgment, all indicate that we are not *supposed* to judge. It is an error as well to think that Roland regrets his act and repents before he dies. If he were truly to repent, it would have to mean that his act—his refusal to summon help—was free of all necessity; in that case he could not be an epic hero, and he would become the proper victim of the audience's common sense. For the moment we think that he should have acted otherwise, we deny the force of necessity. If there is no necessity, there is no providence; and if there is no providence, then Roland's heroism becomes an aberration, a state of madness, a terrible display of the private will gone berserk. Only from one point of view—Roland's own—is his choice completely free. From the perspective of the poem's audience, he *had* to do what he did, for the battle of Rencesvals was now locked into the great design of history—the glorious history of France. From that perspective, the action he takes is necessary, preestablished; and Roland's greatness lies in his willingness to carry it out. We are moved by his warrior's rapture as he speaks of the duties of the vassal, not because we share his notion of loyalty, but because we see his notion of loyalty leading him to fulfill the role into which, from the audience's point of view, history has already cast him.

Roland explains why he refuses to summon help: he says that to do so would bring shame upon himself, upon his family, and upon France. He also gives the reasons *why* it would bring shame. He believes that it is his duty to fight alone: that is why the poem makes him twice speak the famous passage on the vassal's duty at this moment. He is also sure that he can win, and it would be shameful to summon help when he and his men can defeat the Saracens alone, for he had sworn that Charles would not lose a single man, not a horse or a mule, as the army made its way through the passes.[18] The concerns that led him to refuse to summon help—honor, lineage, sweet France—are named and praised by Charles, later, in his lament for Roland. These are the lights by which Roland acts. But we, the audience, enlightened by necessity, can see more: if Roland calls for help and Charles returns, the battle will lose its judicial character.[19] Only if there is a victory of the few against the many can the outcome of the battle reveal the will of God. If Roland is right, then God has bestowed upon his outlook a special grace. He is the agent of God's will, the supreme vassal, and God has sanctified his calling, endowed it with a mission. In this we can detect an historical resonance. When the Church, in the interests of the peace movement and the crusade, set about enlisting the warrior class into its service, it did not try to temper the ferocious instincts of these men but rather attempted to train their martial spirit, in all its savage pride, upon a new, universal, Christian goal.[20]

This may be the best moment to warn against importing twentieth-century sanctities into this 900-year-old poem. The Saracens in *The Song of Roland*, as the fantastic names and the ludicrous creed attributed to them make clear, are the postulated enemies of God, which meant in the Middle Ages that they are the force opposed to all human values. The poem is not, therefore, a genocidal tirade against the civilization of Islam; the Saracens here are demonic reflections, human souls degraded into automatons because they are without God—without reverence and humility. The true faith they lack is the faith of love, the commitment to the human community. Charlemagne naturally looks back to the time of Daniel, his brother-heir; but, except for the fathers who lose their sons, there is no kinship and fidelity among the Saracen generations—they have no past to look back to. They are agents of discontinuity, mad votaries who trample the idols they worship underfoot, who disintegrate the structures they mimic. Compassion for the enemy would be treason to man's community.

But that does not mean that the human reality of the enemy is obliterated in this great poem. Sometimes vehement hatred of another signifies a greater human commitment than pity, for pity often means that one has given up hope for the other's chances and, amid copious tears, written him off. It is said of Baligant that if he had been Christian he would have been a great man, a remark that is often mistaken as an expression of blind intolerance. But it is really an explicit recognition, in the poem's early feudal idiom, of the sec-

ular equality of Christian and pagan, and of the infinitely redeem-
able humanity of the enemy. The pagans are condemned, not be-
cause they are without God, but because they are without God by
their own choice.[21] They have used their heroic powers to thwart
human value, but to their dying breath they have the chance to be
converted by love. That is, as things turn out, a privilege reserved for
Bramimunde alone. The others, if they are not killed by the sword,
are converted by it. The poem's outlook is thus irreconcilable with
the celebration of pluralism characteristic of our enlightenment; but
it also excludes the ultimate nightmare, our nightmare, the vision
that we dread: the tribalism of the industrial age, which regards those
on the far side of the world as alien in essence, morally strange, in-
capable of our humanity.

Each man in this feudal community finds his place in a hierarchi-
cal structure of loyalties that ends in Charlemagne, to whom all are
bound, as he is bound to them in the obligation to protect them.[22]
Each of the barons holds a position with respect to his own men—
the men he brought with him to battle—analogous to that of Charles
with respect to the great barons and ultimately to the whole commu-
nity. The men are bound to the lord, the lord to Charlemagne. The
word "man," *hume*, is a technical term here, designating the sworn
vassal, one who has done homage to a lord in exchange for protec-
tion, nurture, and gifts. The relation that binds man and lord, and
man and man, in this way is designated *amur*, love; so that when
Ganelon, at the height of his rage, shouts at Roland: *Jo ne vus aim
nïent* (306), "I do not love you," that is no understated and ironical
insult but the most terrible thing he could utter. It means: the bonds
of loyalty are cut, we are enemies. It is a *desfiance*, a withdrawal of
faith, a declaration of war, and, in the feudal age, it legalized
revenge. This is a point on which Ganelon pins his life at his trial.

We can see here how the poem depicts Ganelon always as a con-
scientious follower of the law and of the oldest feudal values. One of
the many instances of perfect feudal love (in the sense defined above)
occurs in the scene in which Ganelon parts from his men to go on
his mission to the Saracens. Here we see the deportment of true vas-
sals and a true lord: they beg to accompany him, he refuses to endan-
ger their lives recklessly and provides for the succession of his son
and the peace of his realm in the event of his death. And here we see
as well the true Ganelon, the essential Ganelon—the man who, in
his whole-hearted obedience to the law, subverts its intention and
works the destruction of his community. For the effect of his brave
departure is to sow the seeds of discord and to endanger the life of
Charles's greatest vassal (lines 342ff). Ganelon the traitor is a pure
creature of convention: his every word and deed are preceded by a

passage indicating how someone regards him and what someone expects of him, and everything he does or says confirms that description and fulfills those expectations. [23] Depending on who describes or observes him, he is a raging malcontent, a faithful vassal, a false counselor, a revered lord of ancient lineage and long service, a liar, a protector. Note the utter inconsequence of his bringing up Basile and Basan (line 330) after he had argued in favor of accepting Marsilion's offer of peace. In recalling their memory he is restating a point made earlier by Roland (lines 207–10). He has completely reversed himself. His successive states of character are bewildering, all the more striking in comparison with the consistency of his effect: he is continually programed and reprogramed, and invariably destructive. Only in the trial is he named and defined forever.

The fact that Ganelon, the traitor, is repeatedly depicted as the perfect lord and vassal is eloquent testimony to the secret, indwelling weakness of the structure over which Charles presides. Ganelon never breaks any rules:* he sees himself, and rightly so, as an upholder of the most venerable law, the earliest bonds of human community. In his first outburst against Roland, he denounces his stepson for putting a kinsman in danger and thus breaking an ancient and prefeudal bond. And yet, Ganelon is a traitor. *In fact, it is by following the rules that Ganelon commits his treason.* That is the unspeakable wonder of Ganelon: he betrays his land by conforming to its law.

He denies with his last breath that he committed treason and insists that what he did was legal. This argument is no courtroom trick. His sincerity and the authenticity of his claim are reflected in the truly admiring portrait that the poet inserts at this moment (3762–64); in the admiration of his peers; in the unwillingness of his judges to condemn him, intimidated as they are by Pinabel, who will fight for him in the trial by battle and whose immense strength reflects the strength of Ganelon's position; in his status as a noble lord of a great and ancient family. He is no outsider, no Sinon, but an authentic member of this society and a passionate believer in its original law. He claims that revenge was his right and that he had fulfilled all of the established prescriptions by which revenge is sanctioned. "I took vengeance," he says; "I'll admit to no treason in that." For the right to take revenge is a basic right in the feudal community ruled by

---

* With one exception: he lies to Charlemagne about the death of the Algalife (lines 681–91), a clear act of treason for which he deserves to die. And yet, nothing more is ever said about it. In his indictment of Ganelon, Charles never mentions it. The poet wants Ganelon's treason and the justice of his execution to be beyond question to the audience; but he does not want the trial to be affected by this evidence, which, if it were mentioned, would have made the rest of the trial and especially the judicial combat unnecessary. The poet wants the trial to hinge on a completely different issue.

Charles, the oldest sanction of justice. Now the trial must determine whether there is a higher right than vengeance.[24]

In the grandeur, sincerity, and persuasiveness of Ganelon is reflected the weakness of the entire system, for Ganelon, as he sees it, did nothing more than what the system authorized. And he is right; nobody had ever imagined the things their covenant could sanction. It is a fact that Ganelon could never have committed his treason had he lacked what the system provided and his own honored place within it. From his native status and his adherence to the law arises his treason. Without due process, without the prescriptions of custom, without a communal heritage of ethics and rights (as, for example, the right to take revenge), without those conventions that preserve the life of a community, Ganelon would have lacked the means to betray his native land. He is therefore the arch-traitor, for through him the system betrays itself. Ganelon plays an essential role in this system: he is its traitor. He brings to pass the unsuspected consequences of its fundamental laws, endows it with a shadow. For his presence is as necessary as the shadow cast by a body: if a body exists, its shadow necessarily exists; without the shadow there can be no body. Without the traitor or the traitorous force, there can be no system. In Ganelon we see, not a man who for one reason or another—rage, disaffection, avarice—*becomes* a traitor, but a man who was a traitor from the very beginning, a traitor by necessity, whose destructiveness is uncaused because his essence precedes every cause. For what can be the cause of his treason? It is true that Roland provoked him; one may even believe Ganelon's assertion that Roland cheated him—and these would be sufficient causes if Ganelon were only an avenger. But he is something more—the trial proves it: he is a *traitor*, and no motive conceivable in the poem explains that. His uncaused act can accommodate every cause conceivable in the feudal world. The mystery of his treason is a sign of his elemental being.

Ganelon is the destructive element of every secular structure, the indwelling cause of its instability. In him we recognize the traitorous possibility of every institution. Custom can betray, because it can preserve and reinforce an evil. The law can betray, because it can show the criminal how to commit a crime and be acquitted. Even loyalty can betray, because the object of one's loyalty may obscure higher values: Ganelon keeps faith with his family and his ethical code and just for that reason cannot see the supreme good of the Emperor's mission or the rights of the community sworn to fulfilling it. Praise of one's comrades, the longing for peace, piety itself can betray.

Ganelon's treason reveals that the precious rights and customs of every community will tear it to pieces if they are not hierarchized. Some rights have precedence over others, and the right of the King in fulfilling his God-given role has precedence over all. This is a hard-won principle, for according to the poem, no conflict had brought it down to earth before this, and it is not articulated until the trial, at the very end, by one man—"not too tall, not too short"—a man whose eloquence lies in his lack of personal brilliance and his willingness to stake his life on that principle. And still no one sees the principle, save Charles and his man: the barons do not see it, they are blind and filled with panic before the grandeur of Ganelon's lineage and the strength of Pinabel. They are reasonable, moderate, forgiving, and therefore almost traitors themselves (line 3814), for they do not know what is at stake—they bear no scars, they cannot see, they did not witness the martyrdom at Rencesvals. It takes the hand of God in the battle between Charles's properly nondescript man and the mighty and beautiful Pinabel to reveal the truth: the right of the King precedes all others.

Through the crime of its native-born traitor, the system has discovered its essential weakness, and a better system has emerged, the system of Charlemagne's great Christian empire. The grave losses caused by Ganelon's treason are redeemed, transformed into the precious suffering of rebirth, the moment he is declared a traitor. For a new state is brought into being by the treason of Ganelon, which appears as a shadow-act of the great treason that inaugurated the salvation of the human race, and by the trial in which he is condemned. For the first time, the reality of *dulce France* is fully established in the poem: sweet France is what he betrayed. For the first time, France is more than the remote and undefined object of the Christian's love and the Saracens' hate. Here, in the trial of Ganelon, it is involved in the action in the way that the other characters are, both as sufferer and as agent. The trial that defines the identity of Ganelon affirms the existence of a coherent political being, a state, whose presence is now immediate and effective. And this dramatic appearance of the state within the frame of the poem's action comes about for this reason: when something can be betrayed, that is proof that it exists, that it is no longer a mass of disunited powers but a defined being capable of engendering obligations. It can be betrayed because it is real and has the right to demand loyalty. And when this being is the community of a people and its king, then the treason committed against them is proof that they have established the institutions that make up a state; for Ganelon has shown that these institutions are the necessary condition of treason. And further, when this being declares itself betrayed, that is proof that it has become aware of its identity, that an act of self-consciousness, a *prise de conscience*, has taken place. And finally, when the state condemns its traitor, it reveals not only its power as an entity but also the ethical basis of its claim to loyalty: the destruction of the state through treason would be an arch-crime because it would threaten the basis of all human community, of human existence itself. Thus in the same act the state declares its identity and asserts its right to exist.

This is the precious moment for which every other moment in the poem was a preparation. We can recall, for example, the "impotence" and "passivity" of the King when Ganelon names Roland to command the rear-guard. Charles's immobility stems from the fact that he is legally paralyzed: Roland has not been chosen for the rear-guard as Charles's vassal, and so Charles is not in a position, even though he is Roland's lord, to order him to stay or go. Roland is chosen by an assembly of the barons, who, in giving the King their counsel, are acting as representatives of the whole state and, in effect, exercising the authority of the state.[25] That is why the King's weakness at this moment is a preparation for the great trial at the end: the King cannot become strong until an act of treason is declared.

Charles's behavior in this scene is usually interpreted as a reflection of the king's historic position vis-à-vis the barons at the time of the poem's composition. There may be something to that idea, but the full effect of this scene is clear only at the end of the poem. If this scene reflects an historical situation, it does not do so directly, for the barons are not shown acting in their own interests against those of the King. They are acting on a state matter, and Roland is named to perform a service to *all*. That is why it is a tremendous moment when Tierri says to Charles: "Roland was acting in *your* service": for the first time the idea is put forth that service to all is identical with service to Charles, and vice versa, that Charles embodies the interests and authority of the state.

Thus it is only after the trial that it becomes possible to define the meaning of "sweet France" and the principle of its unity. Before that, we get only fleeting glimpses of a certain spirit shared by those who fight in that land's name: the courteousness and companionship of Roland and his comrades, the universal love for Charles, the sumptuousness and concord of the Christian camp. But these impressions are obscured by others: the disagreements in council, the sudden revelations of Charles's weakness, the private feuds, the disintegrative allegiances to family and private interests. The French, when they think of their land, remember their wives and daughters, their fiefs and domains (lines 820f). Thus the expression *France* has a certain effect but no clear definition: Baligant and the other pagans speak with perfect ease of "sweet France."

Before the trial, France was defined only by its outer enemies: the hostility of the Saracens proved that France was *dulce*, pleasing to God, for it was locked in combat with the enemies of God. Now, however, through the condemnation of its native-born traitor,

France takes on a native character and reveals exactly what it is that pleases God: it is a state in which all men are bound in loyalty through their ultimate obligation to the King, a state whose unity and well-being derive from the subordination of all privileges, rights, and interests to the King chosen by God. At the end of the poem Charles receives a new mission as head of a new born state.

Before the treason, when Roland was still alive, the God-given principle of the supremacy of the King was not yet clear, despite his own exemplary loyalty to Charles. Because of Roland's eminence, the greatest reverence could still be given to horizontal obligations—to family loyalties and the demands of personal honor—until Ganelon revealed the disintegrating effect of these unordered rights. But now all is arranged as it is pleasing to God, in a vertical hierarchy that ends, on this earth, in the King.

In other words: after the trial, as the system expunges its essential traitor, it also makes an end of itself: we do not see emerging from the trial the system that had always existed only now in a healthier condition, but rather a different system, something new and nearer to God's intention. Modern readers may be satisfied with an interpretation of the poem as a justification and celebration of a political and religious order. But for the audience that shared its past and its vision of the future, there was more. The action of *The Song of Roland* foreshadows, as we have seen, the great apocalyptic battle and the end of time as prophesied in the Book of Revelation. That last great battle will also be caused by treason, and it will end in the Last Judgment, after which the world will be set right again. Now since Charles's battle against the pagans prefigures that final battle, it must also prefigure that last stage in the restoration of the world: the historical event reveals the eschatological truth. Viewed in this light *The Song of Roland* resembles what Dante calls "the allegory of the theologians," setting forth real events—things that really happened—as a revelation of the last things to come. And when the action of the epic is finally completed, when the historical event has taken place, then the condition of the world is in fact closer to the final eschatological perfection that the event foreshadows.

A new state arises from the destruction wrought by treason. The traitor has used to evil purpose all that was good in his society and has thereby served the good: his treason made the King strong. The poem draws a parallel between the crimes of Ganelon and Judas: an immeasurable good arose from both. Therefore this too, this ultimate service of evil to the good, is foreseen. In John 6:70 Jesus says: *Have not I chosen you twelve, and one of you is a devil?*—and these words filled Saint Augustine with wonder:[26]

He might have said: "I have chosen *eleven*"; is the devil chosen, is the devil among the elect? One speaks of the elect in praise: is that man elect through whom, contrary to his will and without his knowledge, a great good arises? Just as wicked men use God's good works for evil, so God uses the wicked works of men for good. . . . What is more evil than Judas? Among all those who followed the Master, among those twelve, it was to him that money was entrusted and the care of the poor. And then, ungrateful for this great privilege, for so great an honor, he took in money and did away with justice, this dead man betrayed life, turned as an enemy against Him whom he had followed as a disciple. This is the great evil of Judas; but the Lord used his evil for good. He suffered Himself to be betrayed, that He might redeem us: behold the evil of Judas turned into good! How many martyrs has Satan persecuted? And yet had Satan ceased his persecution, we would not this day be celebrating the glorious martyr's crown of Saint Laurentius.

Thus it is foreseen that the traitor must participate in every structure and be the necessary cause of human amelioration. Here again we see that the poem wants its narrative to be judged in the light of providence; and in that light Roland's death is a great victory, and the cause of great good for all—martyrdom and a place among the flowers of Paradise for those who fell, a new state for those who survive and inherit the earth. Of this new state we are permitted to see only the circumstances of its birth and in Tierri its characteristic man. Its essential traitor has not yet appeared: that belongs to another story. And so we are shown a view of human progress, the providential cycle of treason and rebirth, which will come to an end in the conflict between the last traitor, the Antichrist, and the hordes of heaven—the great battle prefigured in the episode of Baligant. Through this painful cycle a small advance has been won, the foundation of a new state, whose good lies in loyalty, or, in the feudal sense, love.

ON METER AND STYLE

Every reader of *The Song of Roland* is struck by its distinctive and unforgettable style: the flat declarativeness of its lines, the dizzying shifts in tense, the absence of an explicit connection between one statement and another, the wholesale repetition of many passages, the frequent restatement of the same idea and retelling of the same event, the thinness of its vocabulary (consisting of fewer than 1800 words) and the rare use of figurative language, the powerful conclusiveness of each *laisse* (each group of lines), which gives one the feeling that the narrative repeatedly comes to an end and then resumes.

The style is a powerful instrument in the hands of the *Roland* poet, a man who works with silences as well as words. We can trace here only a fraction of what he achieves with his strong meter, his formulas, his few words.

Many of the stylistic features mentioned above reflect the poet's use of the techniques of oral poetry—poetry composed as it is being performed, as the poet sings or chants or recites it before a present audience. In the last fifty years a great deal of light has been shed on the technique of oral composition.[27] Here, in abbreviated and simplified form, are some of the main points that bear on the style of our poem.

The performer of oral poetry, who is usually if not always unlettered, does not try to memorize a number of lines already composed, a "text": considering the enormous length of some oral epics, that would be beyond the capacity even of primitive memory. Instead, he uses his memory to retain a great hoard of formulas that have been developed, honed down to perfection, over many generations and that he has learned in the course of a long apprenticeship and professional life. He possesses as well in his trained and capacious memory a great keyboard of narrative elements—longer elements (sometimes called "themes") and shorter elements ("motifs") such as, for example, the scene of the council, the arming of the warrior, the preparation for a journey, the journey itself (often depicted as a quest, a bridal quest or a quest for treasure), the death of the warrior in battle. Depending upon the occasion, the audience, and the length of time at his disposal, the performing poet chooses among the vast range of themes that would be included in the full, unabridged version of his tale. He composes the narrative on the spot, line by line, guided in his choice of incident and formula by the theme; for in his mind each theme is already attached to a particular subgroup of motifs and formulas, and his final choice, in performance, is determined by the narrative and metrical pattern.[28] He does not—could not—compose each line word by word, nor could he choose in each line from the whole, enormous common stock of formulas, for he would be paralyzed in mid-recitation by the sheer quantity of his choices.

In the *Chanson de Roland*, for example, each line consists basically of ten syllables divided by a pause (or caesura) after the fourth syllable (occasionally after the sixth). A formula of four or six syllables will obviously fill out the first or second part of a line. But a formula may also have fewer syllables, in which case it must be so designed that it can be joined to another brief formula to fill out one part of the line (or hemistich). The formula *ço dist li reis* ("the king said this") fills up the first part of the line; and whatever the semantic value of *ço*, it does fill out the meter. If the attribution of speech is to occur in the second part of the line, the formula must contain six syllables: *dist li emperere Carles*. To take another example: *ki a or est gemmee* ("which is set with precious stones in gold") is a frequent and useful second-hemistich formula: it can be applied to different objects (*sun elme*, "his helmet," line 3142; *la bone sele*, "the good saddle," line 1373) and turned around to fit the assonance (*ki est gemmee ad or*, line 1587). It is an essential principle of oral poetry that whenever the same combination of metrical, lexical, semantic, and phonological conditions occurs, the same formula is used: this is the principle of economy or thrift.

The lines are bound by assonance into units called *laisses* (from Latin *lectio*, "reading"), which vary in length, ranging from five to thirty-five lines. Here is *laisse* 34, the caesuras indicated by a space. Certain unstressed syllables (occurring after the last stress in each hemistich) are not to be counted; these are indicated by (—).

1 2   3 4(—)   5 6 7 8   9 10(—)
Li reis Marsílies   ad la culur müee,
King Marsilion   has changed color,

1   2 3 4   5 6   7 8   9 10(—)
De sun algeir   ad la hanste crollee.
he has shaken   the handle of his javelin.

  1   2 3   4(—)   5 6   7 8 9 10(—)
Quant le vit Guenes,   mist la main a l'espee,
When Ganelon saw that,   he set his hand to his sword,

1   2   3   4(—) ·   5 6   7 8   9 10(—)
Cuntre dous deie   l'ad del furrer getee,
he has drawn it   from the sheath about two fingers' length,

1 2 3 4   5   6 7 8 9   10(—)
Si li ad dit: —Mult estes belé è clere!   445
and has said to it: "You are so beautiful and bright!

   1   2 3 4   5   6 7 8   9 10(—)
Tant vus avrai   en curt a rei portee!
How long shall I have held you   in a king's court!
[or: As long as I shall have   held you in a king's court,]

1   2   3 4   5   6 7 8   9 10(—)
Ja ne·l dirat   de France lí èmperere
the Emperor   of France will never say

  1   2 3   4(—)   5   6   7 8   9   10(—)
Que suls i moerge   en l'estrange cuntree;
that I alone died   in this foreign land;

1	2	3	4		5	6	7	8	9	10(—)

Einz vos avrunt   li meillor cumperee.—
rather, [or: before]   the best men (in that land)
                    shall have paid for you."

1	2	3	4		5	6	7	8	9	10(—)

Dïent paien: —Desfaimes la mellee!—   450
Say the pagans: "Let us break up the quarrel!"

The tenth syllable of every line contains the stressed vowel *é* followed by an unstressed *e*. The effect of the inversions (in lines 442, 447, 449, for example) and of the separation of auxiliary and past participle (446, 449), aside from maintaining the assonance, is to induce or reinforce a pause after the fourth syllable. The caesuras are regular and sharply defined. There is no enjambement, every line contains a complete clause; and in the complex sentence that runs from 446 to 449, the succession of clauses is uninterrupted and easily followed, since each clause is assigned to a separate line. The first hemistich usually contains a complete clause or phrase. In all of these respects, this *laisse* is typical of the composition of the entire poem.

Long, periodic sentences occur as well in oral poetry and in other poetry intended for performance. They are usually cast in carefully balanced parallel syntax, clearly mapping out the sentence structure for an audience that listens to (rather than reads) the narrative, an audience for whom each word dies into the air upon being uttered. In the next laisse (35), Ganelon speaks as follows (the translation of the main clause is in capitals):

Jo ne lerreie   por tut l'or que Deus fist
I SHALL NOT FAIL   for all the gold that God made

Ne tut l'aveir   ki seit en cest païs
or for all the wealth   there may be in this land

Que ne li dïe,   se tant ai de leisir,
TO TELL HIM,   if I get the chance to do so,

Que Charlemagnes,   li reis poëstifs,   460
WHAT CHARLEMAGNE, that mighty king,

Par mei li mandet,   sun mortel enemi.
SENDS THROUGH ME TO HIM, his mortal enemy.

Here is a sentence spread out over five lines, and yet for all its length and its intricate pattern—its double asseveration, its conditional clause, its honorific appositives—it responds to the needs of the listening audience. The first suspension of the main clause, for example, consists of two parallel structures, both modifying *lerreie* (*por tut l'or que . . ./ne tut l'aveir ki . . .*), but with mounting intensity, because the first one occupies part of a line, the second an entire line. In the last two lines, the second hemistichs consist of two parallel appositives, each applied to one of the two kings. The presence of the *se*-clause in 459 is determined as much by the rhythm of the whole utterance as by the message it contains. Each element of the main clause occurs in the first hemistich, the second part of the line being reserved for ornament or intensification, so that there is a semantic rhythm that coincides with the metrical pattern.

Nevertheless, it is not only the circumstances of the performance that the poet takes into account here but also the inner demands of the narrative, the need to put into Ganelon's mouth a heroic, grandiloquent utterance of great formality, the result of painstaking calculation. For in this speech we detect his heroic quality—the eloquence of a great baron, the decorum and devotion to duty of a great vassal confronted by violence improperly directed at him on this state occasion—and his cunning as well, his power to manipulate those whom he impresses, as he provokes the Saracens and carries out his plan. And so this speech enacts the implications of every word in the narrative line that introduces this episode: *Mais li quens Guenes se fut ben purpensét* (line 425), "But Ganelon the Count had thought it all out well."

Is *The Song of Roland* an oral poem? Opinion is divided, and the entire question has often—too often—been reduced to a dispute between "traditionalists" (who believe in the continual re-creation of the poem by generations of anonymous poets) and "individualists" (who believe in the unique creation of the poem by a single poet, perhaps named Turold).[29] The extreme individualist position, as we have seen, is now untenable because there is evidence that before the composition of the Oxford *Roland* a legend had developed concerning Roland, his lord, his companions, his betrayer, and his enemies.

Anyone who argues the traditionalist position must insist that the Oxford *Roland* is an oral poem, for otherwise this position is equally untenable: the only kind of poem that develops by slow accretion through many generations is an oral poem, untouched by the definitiveness of a written "text," a poem of continuous potentiality, brought forth anew from the great matrix of formulas and themes each time it is performed—a poem "that lives in variants."[30] Traditionalism therefore regards the Oxford *Roland* as an accident: of the actual and potential variants, which are as infinite and impermanent as the patterns of a continually revolving kaleidoscope, one version (and not necessarily the greatest one ever performed) has chanced to get written down. For there can be no talk of "development" without the assumption of this fluidity. That is why traditionalism must consider the manuscript an anomaly, and it warns us continually against attributing any kind of scriptural authority to it as though it were the "author's" last word:[31]

> . . . the manuscript is a pure accident: it represents nothing more in effect than the recording through writing of some one of the innumerable versions that do not cease being born as long as the song is sung. . . . The manuscript of an individual poet represents an enduring reality, that is, the text fixed by an author; whereas the manuscript of a traditional [i.e. oral] work represents a fleeting moment of a multiform reality.

There are, in fact, other versions of the story of Roland extant, and though these are later than the Oxford poem they are without question based on earlier material and may very well argue the existence of countless other renditions.[32]

Now it is clear that the techniques of oral poetry are at work in the Oxford *Roland*, for part of it is composed by formula and theme. But that does not prove that it is an oral poem. And so the question remains: does the Oxford manuscript contain a copy of a unique creation prepared (not necessarily *written*) in advance of performance; or is it the accidental recording of one performance among a vast number that have been sung into the air? The question is of some importance, for it affects the way we read the poem. If we believe that it was prepared in advance, then we can read it as a "literary" work and respond to its words, images, characters, and events as we do when reading written poetry. We are free to look back, reread, compare part with part, consider what happens to a word or image each time it occurs, study the retroactive effect of one turn of events upon all that has preceded: we respond to the work as a construct designed so that every part affects every other. If we believe that it was composed in performance, then we read it as an oral poem, and we guard against the reader's habit of close reading. If we want to explain why a certain word or image or event is there, we must be careful to remember that it belongs to the theme and to the group of formulas that the theme has attracted: it is there because of the technique of oral composition. We have to block every exegetical impulse; the only context we can refer to is the context of the line—the meter, sound, and sense of ten syllables—and the theme. We must refer every element to a pre-existing, universal, unrestricted repertory of narrative units and fixed expressions, and to the rules governing their use: we must not explain it by some other element in the

poem, especially one that is remote from the local context—that
would be relapsing into our reader's habit.

These are the alternatives that face us if we take a hard line in this
matter. When we come upon the word *martyrie* ("slaughter," "mar-
tyrdom"), for example, should we refer to all the other passages in
which that word appears and consider whether it takes on an added
meaning or an ironic connotation as a result of its frequent recur-
rence? Or should we say that it is there because of the nature of
formulaic poetry, that the poet uses the word each time it occurs, not
because he wants it to reflect upon an earlier use of the word, but
because it fits the meter, the sound pattern, and the narrative mo-
ment and because it is traditionally associated with a certain narra-
tive theme in the field of warfare? If we believe that the poem was
prepared in advance, we refer every element to a system *within* the
poem; if we believe that it was composed in the pressure of perfor-
mance, we refer every element to a system *outside* the poem. That is
the hard line.

Obviously we can never know for sure whether this poem was
prepared in advance or composed on the spot. There is, however,
one thing that is sure: if we make the same demands of this poem
that we would make of a written text, it responds with amazing
beauty. Let us take that same word *martyrie* as an example. If we
bear in mind that it can be used either in the sense of "slaughter" or
in the spiritual sense familiar to us, then we can see that it is often
used with wonderfully illuminating irony. In line 591 Ganelon
warns Marsilion that he must pay a price for the attack on the rear-
guard: *ne·l di por ço, de voz iert la martirie*: "Your men will be mar-
tyred." In betraying the Christian side he still thinks in Christian
terms, and he unintentionally reveals how the pagans are doomed to
die a worse death than the death of the body: they will be "mar-
tyred," but to what cause? In line 965 Margariz boasts of what he will
do to the Christians: *li .xii. per sunt remés en martirie*: "The Twelve
Peers await their *martirie*"; he means "slaughter," but his words con-
tain a truth—the promise held out by Archbishop Turpin of eternal
honor among the flowers of Paradise—that Margariz cannot imag-
ine. In line 1166, Roland says, *cist paien vont grant martirie
querant*: "These pagans seek a great *martirie*." Here one might argue
that, in the context of battle, *martirie* simply means "slaughter,"
without any religious connotations whatever; but this argument, far
from disproving an ironic use of the word, explains what makes it
possible. For if the word did not have a literal and obvious sense to
begin with ("slaughter"), it could not have a second, or ironic,
meaning ("martyrdom"). Roland's words mean that the pagans are
coming to be slaughtered and that they will be "martyrs" to an
unholy cause. The pagans' "martyrdom" is, like the pagans' feudal

system and their apparent virtues—their courage and loyalty—an exact image of the Christian reality, only grounded in error and ending in perdition. In line 1922, on the other hand, Roland uses the word in both senses without any ironic intent: *Ci recevrums martyrie.*

Is it possible that the *Chanson de Roland* came into existence as a written text employing a number of oral formulas and themes? For a long time this possibility was denied: there was no such thing as a "transitional" poet, one who could write and still feel free to make use of the oral-poetic system. A poet was either "oral" or "literary" and would use only the techniques appropriate to his type. But now there is evidence that the *Chanson de Roland* (as well as other medieval epics) was composed precisely in conditions formerly considered impossible.[33] A great poet—"the last redactor"—using material that was preserved in oral tradition (and perhaps by other means as well) composed a text intended for oral delivery. And because this poem was meant to be performed, he used the techniques of oral composition: those were the techniques employed in the poetic material he inherited, as well as in most vernacular poetry, and they were adapted to the entertainment of an attending audience—just as the principles of rhetoric, which began as an oral art, have been preserved and venerated for centuries in written prose. Thus the poet was not bound by the principle of economy and could make use of a wider choice of expressions and techniques than those of purely oral poetry. If this is true, then we should read *The Song of Roland* as words on the page, a literary text.

Nor can we, in fact, read it in any other way. No matter what traditionalists and individualists may say, the alternatives we have been examining are not mutually exclusive. We say that if it is a literary poem, it is prepared in advance; but if it is an oral poem, how can it *not* be prepared in advance? The lettered poet can write several drafts and revise indefinitely. But what does the oral poet do? He *retells* a tale that he has heard and told many times before: every past performance is an earlier draft, and every present performance in effect a revision. The oral poet would, to be sure, find the idea of revision incomprehensible and would swear that he is retelling a story exactly as he has heard it; but we know that in fact he does *not* tell it the same way twice—the very nature of oral poetry rules that out, for that would be tantamount to memorizing a text. He may not intend to alter his narrative, but he does: The effect of his repeated performance of the narrative is to refine and improve his treatment of it.[34] Even if he does not think in terms of making the poem better, even if in most cases he only makes it different, all these distinctions fall when a great poet appears: the line between alteration and revision becomes very faint then, if it exists at all. He knows what he is going to say—the tale is mapped out by themes and the formulas that they attract—and he is free to use a certain word or image or episode now because he knows he will use it or something similar later: *The Song of Roland* is distinguished by this parallelism. The whole song is present to the poet. He therefore has a sense of context similar to the literate reader's. A strictly oral poet would not "revise" as a lettered poet does, for the one composes word by word, the other by groups of words. Nevertheless, what shall we call his refinement of the poem but "revision"? Besides, the "strictly oral poet" is a disputed postulate as far as this poem is concerned. Only about twenty-five percent of the lines of *The Song of Roland* contain word-groups identified beyond question as formulas. A good part of the poem may have been composed with greater freedom. As far as the question of how we should read this poem is concerned, the difference between the two kinds of poetic composition boils down to two issues: the poet's perception of what he was doing, and the conditions in which he worked on the earlier versions—two issues about which we can never have sufficient knowledge and which in any case have no bearing on our response to the poem before us.

Then let us respond to every feature of this poem and not fear that the procedures of its technique can invalidate our response. Every feature affects us in a certain way, and the capacity to produce that response is part of its essential reality. For example, the poem is effectively anonymous: the name Turoldus in the last line may be the name of the poet, or the scribe, or the redactor, or the performer, or the author of the source, and the mystery of his name only intensifies the effect produced by anonymity. Most epic poems from this period are, as it happens, anonymous; but if we rest content with that observation, we imply that the anonymity of *The Song of Roland* is accidental and therefore irrelevant to our response. But in fact it affects us profoundly, just as we are affected by the appropriate mystery of Turoldus' name; and if we define that effect, we shall discover something essential in the poem. For its anonymity reflects its style, and its moral disposition. In our response to the poem, its anonymity is a positive sign of its mode of expression, which is enormously powerful without being in the least idiosyncratic. In that same anonymity we find its ethical bias confirmed: its unconcern with subjective experience, its celebration of a communal heritage, its sense of the mission bestowed upon a people newly chosen in the age of grace, its injunctive force trained with visionary blindness upon all of its audiences—all who hear these words must struggle to restore the kingdom that once pleased God—a force that no man speaking in his own name could ever command.

We may react to this anonymity as we would to an ancient ritual gesture, if we regard it as something that was once ordained and significant, a revelation to a circle of witnesses, the poem's mark of its own authenticity. We are about to hear, not the imaginings of some vainly "original" poet, but a privileged vision of history, beheld long ago by a nation that believed itself called to the service of God. Its anonymity identifies it as something monumental and inherited, with an authority that transcends the credibility of any one person. It is therefore analogous to the anonymity of the Scriptures: it declares that the true author is greater than any man who can be named, the events it narrates are more fraught with meaning than any man can imagine, the truth it reveals is higher than any man can conceive: it is a monument, it belongs to all.

Something needs to be said in this connection about the role that formulas play in epic style, and particularly in the style of *The Song of Roland*. Because they are meant for limitless repetition, formulas do not strive to be brilliant or literary. The more "original" and unexpected any expression is, the less it can bear repetition. The formula has to be honed down, polished, made spare, indivisible, uniform, inconspicuous with regard to its literary merits, serviceable, purified of every element that may restrict it to a single use or a single context or even a single poem. The deathless line belongs to written poetry and usually to an individual talent; moreover, it is not a greater cause for celebration than the true formula, which will keep its force and deliver its message no matter how many times it is repeated. Milton's line "When Charlemain with all his peerage fell / by Fontarabbia" makes us pause in admiration, with that astonishing burst of sound at the end. But our high estimate of this line and of the poet's talent would be utterly wiped out if we found him using it another time, or every time the occasion could accommodate it. *Par amur et par feid*, "in love and loyalty," does not arrest our attention with its brilliance, for the oral poet does not want us to miss the movement of his narrative as we ponder the beauty of his words. The formula gives us the pleasure of feeling a metrical demand fulfilled, the keystone fitting into the place reserved for it. Some of these formulas are certainly beautiful by any standard and would glisten in a work meant for reading; but it is not such beauty that the poet strives for above all—just as individual bricks and stones may have a special glint and texture, though their greatest effect lies in the part they play in the whole structure: whatever that part may be, they must not detach themselves.

It is not enough for a formula to have a certain metrical shape: it has to have as well an indestructible semantic content and ethical integrity. That is one of the reasons why an oral formula sometimes requires generations to perfect: it is an expression that has a certain metrical form and that does not become degraded with repetition. "Don't call us, we'll call you," though it has a good six syllables, is the exact opposite of a formula.

The brilliance with which the *Roland* poet uses the formulaic style has long been celebrated. You hear the same formulas that were used to describe Christian victories now being used to describe pagan victories, and that is frightening (compare lines 1228 and 1576, 1233 and 1578, for example). But the great power of his style cannot be conveyed by such strategies, effective as they are.

We call it a formulaic style even though only about a quarter of the text has been identified beyond question as consisting of formulas. For one thing, it is reasonable to assume that many other expressions are formulas, even though we have not been able to find them used elsewhere. In any case, as far as the style is concerned, this is not a key issue. We may need to know what percent of the text consists of formulas in order to decide whether the *Chanson de Roland* was an oral poem, but we do not need this information in order to see that it is in the *style* of an oral poem. For the only way in which we can identify a word-group as a formula is to find it used elsewhere in the text or in other texts; a formula cannot be distinguished from another word-group in the poem by any other objective standard. If one compares hemistichs identified as formulas with those that are not, one finds no differences in meter, vocabulary, or phonology—*a mun espiét trenchant* (line 867) can be identified as a formula (compare lines 3051, 3114, 3351, and others); *ki ben trenchet et taillet* (1339) cannot, although each word in this group appears several times in the poem. If the *Roland* poet in fact made up wholly new lines, he drew from the same lexical field, he used the same kind of words and constructions that had gone into the making of the formulas.

No matter where he found his lines, the most important thing with respect to his style is that he composed in word-groups rather than single words. Every expression was designed to fit into a four-syllable or a six-syllable mold with a tonic accent at the end, and to be instantly recognized by the audience as part of a traditional motif: when a warrior boasts of what he will do to his enemy, or when he is actually engaged with his companions in bitter combat, something will be said about the sharpness of his spear or the cutting edge of his sword, something familiar and anticipated with pleasure. The technique of composition consisted in molding a grammatical unit—the subject well known to all (*li quens Rollant*), the predicate affirming a famous act (*vait ferir le paien*), the modifier fixing the physical and moral coordinates of the feudal world (*a lei de chevaler*), or any combination of these (*cil sunt prudome*)—into a pre-established metrical form.

The question that concerns us here, therefore, is not whether this or that half-line can be identified as a formula; but given the fact that the entire poem is composed in the style of the formulas, with its metrical demands and its feudal vocabulary, how shall we define the power of that style, and how does the poem make use of that power?

Formulaic language is the refined product of a long tradition and is therefore impersonal, objective, authoritative; it cannot be toyed with or used idiosyncratically. If the theme is war and the motif is the death of the warrior in single combat; and if, when the time comes for the warrior to fall or for his blood to flow, there is a need to define in the first hemistich the direction of this movement, then that need may be filled only with a formula, like *sur l'erbe verte* ("on the green grass"), or a formulaic expression, a word-group that sounds like a formula because its language and structure are the same—in any case not with the kind of surprising and inimitable phrase that we admire in later poetry and identify as the hallmark of a certain poet. In the old epic poem every word-group comes forth as an inevitable expression, both familiar and obligatory, and the property of all.

This was the style prescribed by tradition. And this language, bound as it was by strict rules inherited from the past, was the language of authority, the language reserved for the telling of the nation's history in song. Thus the formulaic style and the historical content of the *chanson de geste*—the great deeds performed by noble ancestors—were inseparable, even indistinguishable. That history was the precious heritage of the feudal community; and apart from charters and documents (like the *Geste Francor* to which the poem refers), it was only the song that preserved the memory of the past; only in its language was the wisdom and greatness of those who came first made available to those who lived now.[35] The words and constructions of the song became the language authorized by tradition for the recital of those great events that revealed the destiny of "sweet France."

Now in using the techniques of oral poetry, Turoldus (if that was the poet's name) was a master of its injunctive and authoritative style. We can see the effect to which he used formulaic language—that is, language that consists of, or emulates, oral formulas—if we recall for a moment our earlier discussion on the nature of epic action. For the power of *The Song of Roland* lies in the relation between necessity and formulaic style.

The formula returns, obeying a law of its own, beyond the pathetic field of the hero's experience: Hector is "tamer of horses" by a rule to which his pains and joys are irrelevant. The blood of the dismembered Ganelon is *li cler sanc*, and it falls *sur l'erbe verte*, as the blood shed by many victims, both pagan and Christian, was bright and famous and flowed upon the green grass. The formula appears according to a transcendent system of versification, whose operations are never affected by the will or the condition of those involved in the process of the action. That system—that strong meter demanding a fixed and venerable expression—cannot take note of any unique or unprecedented experience: it is a system of inflexible word-groups, each of which defines a segment of a universal motif; every fallen warrior's blood flows alike—before the warrior falls, it is already determined how his blood will flow. Every formula occurs, and every newly coined formulaic word-group seems to occur, because the system demands it. That system is therefore one of the structures through which necessity exerts its force. Necessity operates in the appearance of the epithet—the epithet appears because it *must*, because it is, in the light of the system, foreseen.

Every great poet who uses the oral-formulaic technique makes the force of that system his own. As an apparent product of necessity, the epithet reflects, not the action that is going on at any particular moment, but, depending on the context, the glorious stature of the hero as the executor of a providential design, the indispensability of the traitor, the irreplaceable foppery of the king, the fateful compassion of the friend. Hector is "tamer of horses" even when he is being pursued and then transpierced and his body desecrated in the full sight of the family to which he was devoted. The epithet occurring now defines the true freedom of the heroic will—the freedom to chose what necessity decrees—and completely ignores the subjective experience; it continually recasts the sufferer in the role that fate has foreseen for him. His suffering is ordained by the same necessity that chose him as its agent and that now in another mode commands the occurrence of the formula. Now we see him ennobled by necessity: the epithet that celebrates his role transfigures his suffering, associates his pain with his heroic privilege, with the sanctions of a universal order, and prevents his dignity from being obliterated by the spectacle of his undoing.

So, too, the formulas that depict the death of Ganelon come forth, in the work of this great poet, as the result of necessity. The rule that prescribed the four-syllable formula and the six-syllable formula in the line: *Sur l'erbe verte en espant li cler sanc* (3972), corroborates the meaning of the next two lines—

> Guenes est mort cume fel recreant.
> Hom ki traïst altre, nen est dreiz qu'il s'en vant!
> (Ganelon died like a traitor, like one who broke faith.
> When one man betrays another, it is not right that he should live to boast of it!)

None of the hemistichs in these two lines can be positively identified as a formula (they do not occur elsewhere in the poem), but they are strikingly *formulaic*, in the sense that we have defined—the words *fel* and *recreant* and key words throughout the poem; and that last sententious line recalls line 3959: *Ki hume traïst, sei ocit et altroi* ("A traitor brings death, on himself and on others"). Ganelon's death fulfills an ancient and universal injunction: a traitor must be destroyed. Now we see that the execution of Ganelon has taken place by the ultimate authority of a design. The sequence that has led to this event was prescribed, like the long-established order of the words that commemorate it. For necessity operates everywhere: in the death of the traitor, in the singing of the song. The act of treason was necessary, the punishment of the traitor was necessary—the memory, the pattern of the song, the presence of the audience, the mission reaffirmed in the performance, all appear as though foreseen, and they are reflected in the language of necessity, the formulaic style.

We see this again in those remarkable moments when the phrase *dulce France* is uttered by a pagan—Baligant, for example, or Blancandrin. He says *dulce France* because the line demands this formula, but the rule that determines its appearance has all the inexorability of the law that condemns the speaker. In saying *dulce France* he confirms his exclusion from the land of the blessed, his willing enactment of the role assigned to him by providence. The inexorable return of the formula is a mode of necessity, patterned like the action that takes place in the world of the epic.

The demonic stature of Ganelon is revealed through the formulas by which the account of his death is recited. His life and death are foreseen; the evil he did is now located in a divine plan—for this religious resonance is inherent in the formulaic style. The word order of each formula and the rule that determines its use are fixed by the ancient customs of a close-knit people. Now all of these features—the immutable phrasings inherited from a remote past, the revered tradition that prescribes the times when these words must be uttered, the implicit attendance of an initiated audience united by a common heritage, the commemoration of a decisive act in a necessitarian world—are essential features of a sacred text.[36] The formulaic poet stands to the tradition governing his words in a relation formally identical with that of the *scriba Dei* to the divine source of his text; and his performance participates in the nature of a rite. He "makes up" nothing, he does not "choose" his words like the solitary prodigy admired in a later age, he does not own his text: he is the instrument—the authentic voice, the privileged hand—of a higher being and a greater will: the mystic source of community.

The poet may, as we have seen, invert the formula, adjust it, for the sake of the meter and the assonance, but his action is never capricious or arbitrary. It is prescribed, and it is therefore the sanctioned exercise of the words' power. The formulas he uses contain remnants of an earlier stage of his language—utterances once heard in the Land of Fathers, archaic words, old forms that preceded changes in sound and idiom, preserved intact by the immutability of the phrase.[37] *The Song of Roland* contains many echoes of the old language; and this, too, the presence of archaic formulations hallowed by tradition, is characteristic of a sacred text. *The Song of Roland* was the monument of its audience and of all the audiences recalled in each performance, it was the secular scripture of their community.

Each *laisse* was a relic and an oracle, retracing the history and revealing the future of the audience—and of the song as well. It commemorated in its archaic phrases all of the past performances of the poem witnessed by the forebears of the audience, and it confirmed the promise that these same words, fixed as they were forever, would be heard by the descendants of those who now attended. Each *laisse* celebrated the past and the future of the nation and of the song; and so, when it was chanted in the ritual of performance, it reflected upon the nation the immunity to time and the intregrative power of the song, and affirmed the communion of all those who listen, have listened, will listen. For the formulaic *laisse* immobilized time, transformed it into an edifice, a human structure infinite in its accommodation and ordained by providence, in which all the heirs of Charlemagne were assembled. Through the miracle of the singing of the song, their forebears became their companions, the empire of their descendants was restored, Charlmagne was *nostre emperere*.

Therefore, each *laisse* contains not so much the linear narration of a certain act as a meditation upon it, a reflection upon one event from several different points of view (the agent's, the audience's, the providence of conditional necessity) the points in time (the agent's present, the audience's present, the chronicled past, the revealed past, the political future, the apocalyptic future). This can be seen most readily in the *laisses parallèles* and *laisses similaries*—successive *laisses* rooted in the same moment in the narrative[38]—but it is the controlling principle nearly everywhere. The action is rarely advanced in each of these narrative units; even in those *laisses* where there appears to be plenty of action in rigorous sequence, as, for example, in the case of "the epic blow," the narrative is halted, rather than advanced. In lines 1642–51, for example, we follow the path of Roland's fearful blow through the helmet, the nose, the mouth, the teeth, the body, the silver saddle and the battle horse of his enemy. This sequence is described in the present tense. Then the action is chronicled, in the simple past, the doumentary tense: "He slew them both"; and the chronicle line is the only one that advances the narrative.[39] Otherwise, the action is refracted, broken down into its elements, stopped, recollected, and then set into the vast mosaic of the past. For the passages describing "the epic blow" are intended not to advance the action but to reveal the quality of the warrior who strikes.

The *laisse* is therefore a circumspection rather than a narrative, a reminiscence and an anticipation focused upon an action that is often (as, for example in lines 1902–3, when the tense shifts suddenly from present to present perfect) not even, strictly speaking, narrated. Each *laisse* is a lyrical arrest, and this static, meditative, reverential attitude of commemoration is one of the most distinctive features of *The Song of Roland*.

BIBLIOGRAPHY AND NOTES

For an introduction to the poem and its literary and historical background, the following are recommended:

Jules Horrent. *La Chanson de Roland dans les littératures française et espagnole au moyen-âge*. Paris, 1951.
Pierre Le Gentil. *La Chanson de Roland*. 2d ed. Paris, 1967.
———. *The Chanson de Roland*, tr. Frances F. Beer. Cambridge, Mass., 1969.
Martín de Riquer. *Los Cantares de gesta franceses*. Madrid, 1952.
———. *Les Chansons de geste françaises*. 2d ed. tr. Irénée Cluzel. Paris, 1968.
D. Karl Uitti. *Story, Myth, and Celebration in Old French Narrative Poetry, 1050–1200*. Princeton, N.J., 1973.
Eugene Vance. *Reading The Song of Roland*. Englewood Cliffs, N.J., 1970.

Studies of the poem are listed in the standard bibliographies (such as those by Robert Bossuat, Urban T. Holmes, John H. Fisher). A good critical survey of earlier scholarship can be found in the following articles by Albert Junker:

"Stand der Forschung zum Rolandslied," *Germanisch-Romanische Monatsschrift* 37 (1956): 97–144.
"Von der Schönheit des Rolandsliedes (O) im Spiegel neuester Forschung," in *Medium Aevum Romanicum*, Festschrift für Hans Rheinfelder, ed. H. Bihler and A. Noyer-Weidner. Munich, 1963.

For an excellent survey see Joseph J. Duggan, *A Guide to Studies on the Chanson de Roland*; Research Bibliographies and Checklists, 15 (London, 1976). Critical bibliographies of the most recent work on the poem can be found in *The Year's Work in Modern Language Studies*, and especially in the *Bulletin bibliographique de la Société Rencesvals*. A lively and useful review of recent work and

44 · *The Song of Roland*

many important contributions are published by the American-
Canadian branch of the Société Rencesvals in its quarterly, *Olifant*.
On the story of Roland in art, see Rita Lejeune and Jacques Stien-
non, *La Légende de Roland dans l'art du Moyen Age*, 2 vols. (Brus-
sels, 1966); translated by Christine Trollope, *The Legend of Roland
in the Middle Ages* (London and New York, 1971).

1. Translated by Lewis Thorpe in: Einhard and Notker the Stammerer, *Two Lives
of Charlemagne* (Baltimore: Penguin Books, 1969). The translation in the Introduc-
tion is the present writer's.
2. For a full account of the incidents of 777–78, see Jules Horrent, "La Bataille des
Pyrénées de 778," *Le moyen-âge*, 78 (1972), 197–227. See also Martín de Riquer,
Chansons (see Bibliography, above), pp. 13–21; and Paul Aebischer, *Préhistoire et
protohistoire du Roland d'Oxford* (Berne, 1972), pp. 13–92.
3. For a survey of all the documentary evidence concerning the development of the
story of Rencesvals, see the works listed above by Martín de Riquer and Jules Horrent;
and Ramón Menéndez Pidal, *La Chanson de Roland et la tradition épique des
Francs*, 2d ed., tr. I.-M. Cluzel (Paris, 1960).
4. de Riquer, *Chansons*, p. 88.
5. See Robert Folz, *Le Souvenir et la légende de Charlemagne dans l'Empire ger-
manique médiéval* (Paris, 1950); Heinrich Hoffman, *Karl der Grosse im Bilde der
Geschichtsschreibung des frühen Mittelalters* (Berlin, 1919).
6. See Erich Köhler, "Conseil des barons" und "Jugement des barons": Epische
Fatalität und Feudalrecht im altfranzösischen Rolandslied* (Heidelberg, 1968); Bar-
naby C. Keeney, *Judgement by Peers* (Cambridge, Mass., 1949); Jean-François Le-
marignier, *Le gouvernement royal aux premiers temps capétiens (987–1108)* (Paris,
1965). See also Karl-Heinz Bender, *König und Vasall* (Heidelberg, 1967).
7. See Matthias Waltz, *Rodlandslied-Wilhelmslied-Alexiuslied, zur Struktur und
geschichtlichen Bedeutung* (Heidelberg, 1965), p. 24.
8. See Karl Heisig, "Die Geschichtsmetaphysik des Rolandsliedes und ihre Vorge-
schichte," *Zeitschrift für romanische Philologie*, 55 (1935), 1–87; and Michael Wendt,
Der Oxforder Roland (Munich, 1970), pp. 170ff.
9. See George Fenwick Jones, *The Ethos of the Song of Roland* (Baltimore, 1963),
p. 121.
10. See Herman Gräf, "Der Parallelismus im Rolandslied," dissertation Julius-
Maximilians-Universität, Würzburg (Wertheim a. M., 1931); Wendt, *Der Oxforder
Roland*, pp. 179–211.
11. See Paul Rousset, "La croyance en la justice immanente à l'époque féodale,"
Le moyen-âge, 54 (1948), 225ff.
12. See, for example, the interesting debate among Larry S. Crist, Wolfgang G.
van Emden, and William W. Kibler in the 1974 and 1975 volumes of *Olifant*.
13. Joachim Bumke, *Wolframs Willehalm* (Heidelberg, 1959), pp. 57ff. Compare
Hans Robert Jauss, "Chanson de geste et roman courtois au XIIe siècle," in *Chanson
de Geste und höfischer Roman*, Heidelberger Kolloquium, January 30, 1961 (Heidel-
berg, 1963), pp. 61–77; translated by the present writer.
14. Menéndez Pidal, *La Chanson de Roland*, p. 504.
15. See Karl-Joseph Steinmeyer, *Untersuchung zur allegorischen Bedeutung der
Träume im altfranzösischen Rolandslied* (Munich, 1963); W. G. van Emden, "An-
other Look at Charlemagne's Dreams in the Chanson de Roland," *French Studies* 28
(1974): 257–71.
16. Compare Bruce A. Rosenberg, *Custer and the Epic of Defeat* (University Park,
Pa., and London, 1974).
17. See Menéndez Pidal, *La Chanson de Roland*, pp. 165ff, especially 167.

18. See lines 755ff, 790ff, 806; Menéndez Pidal, *La Chanson de Roland*, p. 432.
19. See Wendt, *Der Oxforder Roland*, pp. 281ff.
20. See Waltz, *Rolandsliedslied*, pp. 110ff; L. C. Macinney, "The People and Public Opinion in the Eleventh-Century Peace Movement," *Speculum*, 5 (1930), 181–206. The peace movement led by the Church was an attempt to get the nobles to stop fighting among themselves.
21. Uitti, (see Bibliography, above), p. 99.
22. See F. L. Ganshof, *Feudalism*, trans. Philip Grierson, 2d English ed. (New York: Harper Torchbooks, 1961).
23. See Frederick Goldin, "Die Rolle Ganelons und das Motiv der Worte," *Zeitschrift für romanische Philologie*, forthcoming.
24. See Bender, *König und Vasall*, p. 33f.
25. See Köhler, "*Jugement des Barons.*"
26. Saint Augustine, *Tractatus CXXIV in Joannis Evangelium*, Tractatus XXVII, P. L. 1619f.
27. See the following works: Milman Parry, *The Making of Homeric Verse: The Collected Papers of Milman Parry*, ed. Adam Parry (Oxford, 1971).

Jean Rychner, *La Chanson de geste: Essai sur l'art épique des jongleurs* (Geneva and Lille, 1955).

Albert B. Lord, *The Singer of Tales* (Cambridge, Mass., 1960); reprinted in paperback by Atheneum, New York, 1973.

Stephen G. Nichols, Jr., *Formulaic Diction and Thematic Composition in the Chanson de Roland* (Chapel Hill, N.C., 1961).

Joseph J. Duggan, *The Song of Roland: Formulaic Style and Poetic Craft* (Berkeley, Los Angeles, London, 1973).

Edward A. Heinemann, "Composition stylisée et technique littéraire dans la *Chanson de Roland*," *Romania*, 94 (1973), 1–28. See also the same author's review of Duggan's book in *Olifant*, 1 (October 1973), 23–31.

John Miletich, "The Quest for the 'Formula': A Comparative Reappraisal," *Modern Philology*, 74 (November 1976), 111–23. See also the same author's article, "Narrative Style in Spanish and Slavic Traditional Narrative Poetry: Implications for the Study of the Romance Epic," in *Olifant*, 2 (December 1974), 109–128.
28. See Lord, *Singer of Tales*, p. 95.
29. See Italo Siciliano, *Les Origines des chansons de geste*, tr. P. Antonetti (Paris, 1951). The monumental statement of the individualist position is the four-volume work by Joseph Bédier, *Les Légendes épiques*, published in Paris from 1926 to 1929. This remains a vital and indispensable work, though the argument has lost credit. One should also consult his *Commentaires* to his translation of the poem, published in Paris in 1927.
30. A poem *"that lives in variants:"* this phrase is taken from the title of Chapter 2, "Une poésie qui vit de variantes," of the work by Menéndez Pidal, *La Chanson de Roland*.
31. Ibid., p. 63f.
32. The only other assonanced version is contained in a manuscript in the library of San Marco in Venice, designated V4. Written in a mixture of French and Italian, the manuscript dates from the fourteenth century, though the composition of the poem is much earlier. In its first 3845 lines this version is close to the first 3681 lines of the Oxford version; it then goes on to relate other episodes to the end, line 6011.

There are, in addition, seven rimed versions (of which two are fragmentary) dating from the end of the twelfth and the thirteenth century. These versions recast the old song into rimed couplets and expand the material, adding much that betrays the influence of the courtly romance.

There were also translations and recensions of various versions of the story into German, Norse, Welsh, English, Dutch, Spanish, and other languages. Of these, the greatest is the *Ruolandes liet* of Pfaffe Konrad, composed either in the 1130s or around

1170 (each date has its defenders). For an account of all of the versions of the story of Roland, see de Riquer, *Chansons* (see Bibliography, above), pp. 52–59.

33. See Rudy S. Spraycar, "*La Chanson de Roland:* An Oral Poem?" *Olifant*, 4 (1976), 63–74. For a balanced and thorough examination of this question, see Maurice Delbouille, "Les chansons de geste et le livre," in *La technique littéraire des chansons de geste*, Actes du Colloque de Liége, Bibliothèque de la Faculté de Philosophie et Lettres de l'Université de Liège, Fascicule 150 (Paris, 1959), pp. 295–407.

34. See Lord, *Singer of Tales*, pp. 25ff.

35. On oral poetry as a system for preserving and retrieving the wisdom of the past, see Walter J. Ong, S.J., "World as View and World as Event," *American Anthropologist*, 71, 4 (August 1969), 634–47, especially pp. 638–641 and the bibliography at the end of the article.

36. See Paul Zumthor, *Langue et techniques poétiques à l'époque romane (XIe–XIIIe siècles)* (Paris, 1963), pp. 27–69.

37. See Robert A. Hall, Jr., "Linguistic Strata in the *Chanson de Roland*," *Romance Philology*, 13 (1959–60), 156–61.

38. In the *laisses similaires* (for example, *laisses* 40–42, 83–85), the action stops completely; in the *laisses parallèles* (for example, *laisses* 71–78, 93–95, 96–103, 218–225, 232–34), the action is advanced. See Rychner, *La chanson de geste*, pp. 83–107.

39. Exceptionally beautiful examples of this process of chronicling and laudation are in lines 2083–93, and 1678–85. See Frederick Goldin, "Le noyau temporel de la laisse dans la *Chanson de Roland*," forthcoming in the *Actes* of the Eighth Congress of the Société Internationale Rencesvals.

A Note on the Translation

The text used for this translation is the following: Cesare Segre, ed., *La Chanson de Roland, edizione critica*, Documenti di Filologia, 16 (Milan and Naples: Riccardo Ricciardi, 1971). All citations in the notes refer to this edition.

As a rule, meanings implicit in the text have been made explicit in the translation; and very often a single word in the original has been rendered by two or more words. The translation generally follows the tense of the original, except when there would have been too great an offense against English idiom. Again for reasons respecting English idiom, the original present perfect is often translated as a simple past. With few exceptions, the names of places and characters appear as they do in the original: may they continue to inspire wonder, or laughter, or dread. Here and there one line of the original appears as two lines in the translation; in such cases the second line is indented.

Some attempt has been made to preserve the rhythm of the original. There is usually a pause after the fourth or the sixth syllable, and the last unstressed syllable in each hemistich is usually not counted. Obviously, it was never intended that any line should come through as a perfect iambic pentameter. There are many lines that do not fit the basic pattern of four-plus-six or six-plus-four, as the reader will notice, but not as many as there may seem to be at first sight, particularly if the reader is willing to help out sometimes by eliding when one vowel follows another or in such constructions as "it is, that is"; and by reading certain words (such as Marsilion) sometimes as three and sometimes as four syllables.

The way in which a work is presented to the public is a vital part of the context in which one must interpret the words. This translation is based on the fact that the *Chanson de Roland* was meant to be performed before an audience.

All of these remarks are by way of saying that the translation is literal in the following sense: there is nothing in it that is not present, implicitly or explicitly, in the original. This gives the translator a loophole a mile wide. But to translate strictly according to the letter—to ignore what is there simply because it is not there in black and white—is to be guilty of a crime against the poem not unlike Ganelon's against the state.

the song of roland

The Song of Roland

1.

CHARLES THE KING, our Emperor, the Great,
has been in Spain for seven full years,
has conquered the high land down to the sea.
There is no castle that stands against him now,
no wall, no citadel left to break down—   5
except Saragossa, high on a mountain.
King Marsilion holds it, who does not love God,
who serves Mahumet and prays to Apollin.
He cannot save himself: his ruin will find him there. AOI.

2.

King Marsilion was in Saragossa.   10
He has gone forth into a grove, beneath its shade,
and he lies down on a block of blue marble, *concia!* ,
twenty thousand men, and more, all around him. *won't make it*
He calls aloud to his dukes and his counts: *to lend of poem*
"Listen, my lords, to the troubles we have.   15
The Emperor Charles of the sweet land of France
has come into this country to destroy us.
I have no army able to give him battle,
I do not have the force to break his force.
Now act like my wise men: give me counsel,   20
save me, save me from death, save me from shame!"
No pagan there has one word to say to him
except Blancandrin, of the castle of Valfunde.

9. **AOI**: these three mysterious letters appear at certain moments throughout the text,
180 times in all. No one has ever adequately explained them, though every reader
feels their effect.

3.

One of the wisest pagans was Blancandrin,
brave and loyal, a great mounted warrior,   25
a useful man, the man to aid his lord;
said to the King: "Do not give way to panic.
Do this: send Charles, that wild, terrible man,
tokens of loyal service and great friendship:
you will give him bears and lions and dogs,   30
seven hundred camels, a thousand molted hawks,
four hundred mules weighed down with gold and silver,
and fifty carts, to cart it all away:
he'll have good wages for his men who fight for pay.
Say he's made war long enough in this land: 35
let him go home, to France, to Aix, at last—
come Michaelmas you will follow him there,
say you will take their faith, become a Christian,
and be his man with honor, with all you have.
If he wants hostages, why, you'll send them,   40
ten, or twenty, to give him security.
Let us send him the sons our wives have borne.
I'll send my son with all the others named to die.
It is better that they should lose their heads
than that we, Lord, should lose our dignity   45
and our honors—and be turned into beggars!" AOI.

4.

Said Blancandrin: "By this right hand of mine
and by this beard that flutters on my chest,
you will soon see the French army disband,
the Franks will go to their own land, to France.   50
When each of them is in his dearest home,
King Charles will be in Aix, in his chapel.
At Michaelmas he will hold a great feast—
that day will come, and then our time runs out,
he'll hear no news, he'll get no word from us.   55
This King is wild, the heart in him is cruel:
he'll take the heads of the hostages we gave.
It is better, Lord, that they lose their heads
than that we lose our bright, our beautiful Spain—
and nothing more for us but misery and pain!"   60
The pagans say: "It may be as he says."

36. **Aix**: Aachen (Aix-la-Chapelle), capital of Charlemagne's empire.

37. **Michaelmas**: either September 29 or October 16.

5.

King Marsilion brought his counsel to end,
then he summoned Clarin of Balaguét,
Estramarin and Eudropin, his peer,
and Priamun, Guarlan, that bearded one,   65
and Machiner and his uncle Maheu,
and Joüner, Malbien from over-sea,
and Blancandrin, to tell what was proposed.
From the worst of criminals he called these ten.
"Barons, my lords, you're to go to Charlemagne;   70
he's at the siege of Cordres, the citadel.
Olive branches are to be in your hands—
that signifies peace and humility.
If you've the skill to get me an agreement,
I will give you a mass of gold and silver   75
and lands and fiefs, as much as you could want."
Say the pagans: "We'll benefit from this!" AOI.

6.

Marsilion brought his council to an end,
said to his men: "Lords, you will go on now,
and remember: olive branches in your hands;   80
and in my name tell Charlemagne the King
for his god's sake to have pity on me—
he will not see a month from this day pass
before I come with a thousand faithful;
say I will take that Christian religion   85
and be his man in love and loyalty.
If he wants hostages, why, he'll have them."
Said Blancandrin: "Now you will get good terms." AOI.

7.

King Marsilion had ten white mules led out,
sent to him once by the King of Suatilie,   90
with golden bits and saddles wrought with silver.
The men are mounted, the men who brought the message,
and in their hands they carry olive branches.
They came to Charles, who has France in his keeping.
He cannot prevent it: they will fool him. AOI.   95

8.

The Emperor is secure and jubilant:
he has taken Cordres, broken the walls,
knocked down the towers with his catapults.
And what tremendous spoils his knights have won—
gold and silver, precious arms, equipment.   100
In the city not one pagan remained
who is not killed or turned into a Christian.
The Emperor is in an ample grove,
Roland and Oliver are with him there,
Samson the Duke and Ansëis the fierce,   105
Geoffrey d'Anjou, the King's own standard-bearer;
and Gerin and Gerer, these two together always,
and the others, the simple knights, in force:
fifteen thousand from the sweet land of France.
The warriors sit on bright brocaded silk;   110
they are playing at tables to pass the time,
the old and wisest men sitting at chess,
the young light-footed men fencing with swords.
Beneath a pine, beside a wild sweet-briar,
there was a throne, every inch of pure gold.   115
There sits the King, who rules over sweet France.
His beard is white, his head flowering white.
That lordly body! the proud fierce look of him!—
if someone should come here asking for him,
        there'd be no need to point out the King of France.
The messengers dismounted, and on their feet   120
they greeted him in all love and good faith.

9.

Blancandrin spoke, he was the first to speak,
said to the King: "Greetings, and God save you,
that glorious God whom we all must adore.
Here is the word of the great king Marsilion: 125
he has looked into this law of salvation,
wants to give you a great part of his wealth,
bears and lions and hunting dogs on chains,
seven hundred camels, a thousand molted hawks,
four hundred mules packed tight with gold and silver,   130
and fifty carts, to cart it all away;
and there will be so many fine gold bezants,
you'll have good wages for the men in your pay.
You have stayed long—long enough!—in this land,
it is time to go home, to France, to Aix.   135
My master swears he will follow you there."
The Emperor holds out his hands toward God,
bows down his head, begins to meditate. AOI.

10.

The Emperor held his head bowed down;
never was he too hasty with his words: 140
his custom is to speak in his good time.
When his head rises, how fierce the look of him;
he said to them: "You have spoken quite well.
King Marsilion is my great enemy.
Now all these words that you have spoken here—   145
how far can I trust them? How can I be sure?"
The Saracen: "He wants to give you hostages.
How many will you want? ten? fifteen? twenty?
I'll put my son with the others named to die.
You will get some, I think, still better born.   150
When you are at home in your high royal palace,
at the great feast of Saint Michael-in-Peril,
the lord who nurtures me will follow you,
and in those baths—the baths God made for you—
my lord will come and want to be made Christian."   155
King Charles replies: "He may yet save his soul." AOI.

11.

Late in the day it was fair, the sun was bright.
Charles has them put the ten mules into stables.
The King commands a tent pitched in the broad grove,
and there he has the ten messengers lodged;   160
twelve serving men took splendid care of them.
There they remained that night till the bright day.
The Emperor rose early in the morning,
the King of France, and heard the mass and matins.
And then the King went forth beneath a pine,   165
calls for his barons to complete his council:
he will proceed only with the men of France. AOI.

152. **Saint Michael-in-Peril**: The epithet "in peril of the sea" was applied to the
famous sanctuary of Saint Michael on the Normandy coast because it could only be
reached on foot at low tide, and pilgrims were endangered by the incoming tide; even-
tually the phrase was applied to the saint himself.

12.

The Emperor goes forth beneath a pine,
calls for his barons to complete his council:
Ogier the Duke, and Archbishop Turpin,   170
Richard the Old, and his nephew Henri;
from Gascony, the brave Count Acelin,
Thibaut of Reims, and his cousin Milun;
and Gerer and Gerin, they were both there,
and there was Count Roland, he came with them,   175
and Oliver, the valiant and well-born;
a thousand Franks of France, and more, were there.
Ganelon came, who committed the treason.
Now here begins the council that went wrong. AOI.

13.

"Barons, my lords," said Charles the Emperor,   180
"King Marsilion has sent me messengers,
wants to give me a great mass of his wealth,
bears and lions and hunting dogs on chains,
seven hundred camels, a thousand molting hawks,
four hundred mules packed with gold of Araby,   185
and with all that, more than fifty great carts;
but also asks that I go back to France:
he'll follow me to Aix, my residence,
and take our faith, the one redeeming faith,
become a Christian, hold his march lands from me.   190
But what lies in his heart? I do not know."
And the French say: "We must be on our guard!" AOI.

---

190. **March:** a frontier province or territory.

14.

The Emperor has told them what was proposed.
Roland the Count will never assent to that,
gets to his feet, comes forth to speak against it;   195
says to the King: "Trust Marsilion—and suffer!
We came to Spain seven long years ago,
I won Noples for you, I won Commibles,
I took Valterne and all the land of Pine,
and Balaguer and Tudela and Seville.   200
And then this king, Marsilion, played the traitor:
he sent you men, fifteen of his pagans—
and sure enough, each held an olive branch;
and they recited just these same words to you.
You took counsel with all your men of France;   205
they counseled you to a bit of madness:
you sent two Counts across to the Pagans,
one was Basan, the other was Basile.
On the hills below Haltille, he took their heads.
They were your men. Fight the war you came to fight!   210
Lead the army you summoned on to Saragossa!
Lay siege to it all the rest of your life!
Avenge the men that this criminal murdered!" AOI.

15.

The Emperor held his head bowed down with this,
and stroked his beard, and smoothed his mustache down,   215
and speaks no word, good or bad, to his nephew.
The French keep still, all except Ganelon:
he gets to his feet and come before King Charles,
how fierce he is as he begins his speech;
said to the King: "Believe a fool—me or   220
another—and suffer! Protect your interest!
When Marsilion the King sends you his word
that he will join his hands and be your man, *mahedant*
and hold all Spain as a gift from your hands
and then receive the faith that we uphold—   225
whoever urges that we refuse this peace,
that man does not care, Lord, what death we die.
That wild man's counsel must not win the day here—
let us leave fools, let us hold with wise men!" AOI.

Roland

223: **He will join his hands:** Part of the gesture of homage; the lord enclosed the
joined hands of his vassal with his own hands.

16.

And after that there came Naimon the Duke—   230
no greater vassal in that court than Naimon—
said to the King: "You've heard it clearly now,
Count Ganelon has given you your answer:
let it be heeded, there is wisdom in it.
King Marsilion is beaten in this war,   235
you have taken every one of his castles,
broken his walls with your catapults,
burnt his cities and defeated his men.
Now when he sends to ask you to have mercy,
it would be a sin to do still more to him.   240
Since he'll give you hostages as guarantee,
this great war must not go on, it is not right."
And the French say: "The Duke has spoken well." AOI.

17.

"Barons, my lords, whom shall we send down there,
to Saragossa, to King Marsilion?"   245
Naimon replies, "I'll go, if you grant it!
At once, my lord! give me the glove and the staff."
The King replies: "You're a man of great wisdom:
now by my beard, now by this mustache of mine,
you will not go so far from me this year; or ever.   250
Go take your seat when no one calls on you."

18.

"Barons, my lords, whom can we send down there,
to this Saracen who holds Saragossa?"
Roland replies: "I can go there! No trouble!"
"No, no, not you!" said Oliver the Count,   255
"that heart in you is wild, spoils for a fight,
how I would worry—you'd fight with them, I know.
Now I myself could go, if the King wishes."
The King replies: "Be still, the two of you!
Not you, not he—neither will set foot there.   260
Now by this beard, as sure as you see white,
let no man here name one of the Twelve Peers!"
The French keep still, see how he silenced them.

19.

Turpin of Reims has come forth from the ranks,
said to the King: "Let your Franks have a rest.   265
You have been in this land for seven years,
the many pains, the struggles they've endured!
I'm the one, Lord, give me the glove and the staff,
and I'll go down to this Saracen of Spain
and then I'll see what kind of man we have."   270
The Emperor replies to him in anger:
"Now you go back and sit on that white silk
and say no more unless I command it!" AOI.

20.

"My noble knights," said the Emperor Charles,
choose me one man: a baron from my march,   275
to bring my message to King Marsilion."
And Roland said: "Ganelon, my stepfather."
The French respond: "Why, that's the very man!
pass this man by and you won't send a wiser."
And hearing this Count Ganelon began to choke,   280
pulls from his neck the great furs of marten
and stands there now, in his silken tunic,
eyes full of lights, the look on him of fury,
he has the body, the great chest of a lord;
stood there so fair, all his peers gazed on him;   285
said to Roland: "Madman, what makes you rave?
Every man knows I am your stepfather,
yet you named me to go to Marsilion.
Now if God grants that I come back from there,
you will have trouble: I'll start a feud with you,   290
it will go on till the end of your life."
Roland replies: "What wild words—all that blustering!
Every man knows that threats don't worry me.
But we need a wise man to bring the message:
if the King wills, I'll gladly go in your place."   295

21.

Ganelon answers: "You will not go for me. AOI.
You're not my man, and I am not your lord.
Charles commands me to perform this service:
I'll go to Marsilion in Saragossa.
And I tell you, I'll play a few wild tricks   300
before I cool the anger in me now."
When he heard that, Roland began to laugh. AOI.

275. Charlemagne wants them to choose a baron from an outlying region and not one of the Twelve Peers, the circle of his dearest men.

22.

Ganelon sees: *Roland laughing at him!*
and feels such pain he almost bursts with rage,
needs little more to go out of his mind;   305
says to the Count: "I have no love for you,
you *made* this choice fall on me, and that was wrong.
Just Emperor, here I am, before you.
I have one will: to fulfill your command."

23.

"I know now I must go to Saragossa. AOI.   310
Any man who goes there cannot return.
And there is this: I am your sister's husband,
have a son by her, the finest boy there can be,
Baldewin," says he, "who will be a good man.
To him I leave my honors, fiefs, and lands.   315
Protect my son: these eyes will never see him."
Charles answers him: "That tender heart of yours!
You have to go, I have commanded it."

24.

And the King said: "Ganelon, come forward, AOI.
come and receive the staff and the glove.   320
You have heard it: the Franks have chosen you."
Said Ganelon: "Lord, it's Roland who did this.
In all my days I'll have no love for him,
or Oliver, because he's his companion,
or the Twelve Peers, because they love him so.   325
I defy them, here in your presence, Lord."
And the King said: "What hate there is in you!
You will go there, for I command you to."
"I can go there, but I'll have no protector. AOI.
Basile had none, nor did Basan his brother."   330

25.

The Emperor offers him his right glove.
But Ganelon would have liked not to be there.
When he had to take it, it fell to the ground.
"God!" say the French, "What's that going to mean?
What disaster will this message bring us!"   335
Said Ganelon: "Lords, you'll be hearing news."

26.

Said Ganelon: "Lord, give me leave to go,
since go I must, there's no reason to linger."
And the King said: "In Jesus' name and mine,"
absolved him and blessed him with his right hand.   340
Then he gave him the letter and the staff.

27.

Count Ganelon goes away to his camp.
He chooses, with great care, his battle-gear,
picks the most precious arms that he can find.
The spurs he fastened on were golden spurs;   345
he girds his sword, Murgleis, upon his side;
he has mounted Tachebrun, his battle horse,
his uncle, Guinemer, held the stirrup.
And there you would have seen brave men in tears,
his men, who say: "Baron, what bad luck for you!   350
All your long years in the court of the King,
always proclaimed a great and noble vassal!
Whoever it was doomed you to go down there—
Charlemagne himself will not protect that man.
Roland the Count should not have thought of this—   355
and you the living issue of a mighty line!"
And then they say: "Lord, take us there with you!"
Ganelon answers: "May the Lord God forbid!
It is better that I alone should die
          than so many good men and noble knights.
You will be going back, Lords, to sweet France: 360
go to my wife and greet her in my name,
and Pinabel, my dear friend and peer,
and Baldewin, my son, whom you all know:
give him your aid, and hold him as your lord."
And he starts down the road; he is on his way. AOI.   365

28.

Ganelon rides to a tall olive tree,
there he has joined the pagan messengers.
And here is Blancandrin, who slows down for him:
with what great art they speak to one another.
Said Blancandrin: "An amazing man, Charles!   370
conquered Apulia, conquered all of Calabria,
crossed the salt sea on his way into England,
won its tribute, got Peter's pence for Rome:
what does he want from us here in our march?"
Ganelon answers: "That is the heart in him.   375
There'll never be a man the like of him." AOI.

373. **Peter's pence**: a tribute of one penny per house "for the use of Saint Peter," that is, for the Pope in Rome.

29.

Said Blancandrin: "The Franks are a great people.
Now what great harm all those dukes and counts do
to their own lord when they give him such counsel:
they torment him, they'll destroy him, and others."   380
Ganelon answers: "Well, now, I know no such man
except Roland, who'll suffer for it yet.
One day the Emperor was sitting in the shade:
his nephew came, still wearing his hauberk,
he had gone plundering near Carcassonne;   385
and in his hand he held a bright red apple:
'Dear Lord, here, take,' said Roland to his uncle;
'I offer you the crowns of all earth's kings.'
Yes, Lord, that pride of his will destroy him,
for every day he goes riding at death.   390
And *should* someone kill him, we would have peace." AOI.

30.

Said Blancandrin: "A wild man, this Roland!
wants to make every nation beg for his mercy
and claims a right to every land on earth!
But what men support him, if that is his aim?"   395
Ganelon answers: "Why, Lord, the men of France.
They love him so, they will never fail him.
He gives them gifts, masses of gold and silver,
mules, battle horses, brocaded silks, supplies.
And it is all as the Emperor desires: 400
he'll win the lands from here to the Orient." AOI.

31.

Ganelon and Blancandrin rode on until
each pledged his faith to the other and swore
they'd find a way to have Count Roland killed.
They rode along the paths and ways until,   405
in Saragossa, they dismount beneath a yew.
There was a throne in the shade of a pine,
covered with silk from Alexandria.
There sat the king who held the land of Spain,
and around him twenty thousand Saracens.   410
There is no man who speaks or breathes a word,
poised for the news that all would like to hear.
Now here they are: Ganelon and Blancandrin.

32.

Blancandrin came before Marsilion,
his hand around the fist of Ganelon,   415
said to the King: "May Mahumet save you,
and Apollin, whose sacred laws we keep!
We delivered your message to Charlemagne:
when we finished, he raised up both his hands
and praised his god. He made no other answer.   420
Here he sends you one of his noble barons,
a man of France, and very powerful.
You'll learn from him whether or not you'll have peace."
"Let him speak, we shall hear him," Marsilion answers. AOI.

33.

But Ganelon had it all well thought out.   425
With what great art he commences his speech,
a man who knows his way about these things;
said to the King: "May the Lord God save you,
that glorious God, whom we must all adore.
Here is the word of Charlemagne the King: 430
you are to take the holy Christian faith;
he will give you one half of Spain in fief.
If you refuse, if you reject this peace,
you will be taken by force, put into chains,
and then led forth to the King's seat at Aix;   435
you will be tried; you will be put to death:
you will die there, in shame, vilely, degraded."
King Marsilion, hearing this, was much shaken.
In his hand was a spear, with golden feathers.
He would have struck, had they not held him back. AOI.   440

34.

Marsilion the King—his color changed!
He shook his spear, waved the shaft to and fro.
When he saw that, Ganelon lay hand to sword,
he drew it out two fingers from its sheath;
and spoke to it: "How beautiful and bright!   . 445
How long did I bear you in the King's court
before I died! The Emperor will not say
I died alone in that foreign country:
they'll buy you first, with the best men they have!"
The pagans say: "Let us break up this quarrel!"   450

35.

The pagan chiefs pleaded with Marsilion
till he sat down once again on his throne.
The Caliph spoke: "You did us harm just now,
served us badly, trying to strike this Frenchman.
You should have listened, you should have heard him out."   455
Said Ganelon: "Lord, I must endure it.
I shall not fail, for all the gold God made,
for all the wealth there may be in this land,
to tell him, as long as I have breath, all
that Charlemagne—that great and mighty King!—   460
has sent through me to his mortal enemy."
He is buckled in a great cloak of sable,
covered with silk from Alexandria:
he throws it down. Blancandrin picks it up.
But his great sword he will never throw down!   465
In his right fist he grasps its golden pommel.
Say the pagans: "That's a great man! A noble!" AOI.

36.

Now Ganelon drew closer to the King
and said to him: "You are wrong to get angry,
for Charles, who rules all France, sends you this word: 470
you are to take the Christian people's faith;
he will give you one half of Spain in fief,
the other half goes to his nephew: Roland—
quite a partner you will be getting there!
If you refuse, if you reject this peace,   475
he will come and lay siege to Saragossa;
you will be taken by force, put into chains,
and brought straight on to Aix, the capital.
No saddle horse, no war horse for you then,
no he-mule, no she-mule for you to ride: 480
you will be thrown on some miserable dray;
you will be tried, and you will lose your head.
Our Emperor sends you this letter."
He put the letter in the pagan's right fist.

37.

Marsilion turned white; he was enraged;   485
he breaks the seal, he's knocked away the wax,
runs through the letter, sees what is written there:
"Charles sends me word, this king who rules in France:
I'm to think of his anger and his grief—
he means Basan and his brother Basile,   490
I took their heads in the hills below Haltille;
if I want to redeem the life of my body,
I must send him my uncle: the Algalife.
And otherwise he'll have no love for me."
Then his son came and spoke to Marsilion,   495
said to the King: "Ganelon has spoken madness.
He crossed the line, he has no right to live.
Give him to me, I will do justice on him."
When he heard that, Ganelon brandished his sword;
he runs to the pine, set his back against the trunk.   500

38.

King Marsilion went forth into the orchard,
he takes with him the greatest of his men;
Blancandrin came, that gray-haired counselor,
and Jurfaleu, Marsilion's son and heir,
the Algalife, uncle and faithful friend.   505
Said Blancandrin: "Lord, call the Frenchman back.
He swore to me to keep faith with our cause."
And the King said: "Go, bring him back here, then."
He took Ganelon's right hand by the fingers,
leads him into the orchard before the King.   510
And there they plotted that criminal treason. AOI.

39.

Said Marsilion: "My dear Lord Ganelon,
that was foolish, what I just did to you,
I showed my anger, even tried to strike you.
Here's a pledge of good faith, these sable furs,   515
the gold alone worth over five hundred pounds:
I'll make it all up before tomorrow night."
Ganelon answers: "I will not refuse it.
May it please God to reward you for it." AOI.

493. **The Algalife:** the Caliph.

40.

Said Marsilion: "I tell you, Ganelon,   520
I have a great desire to love you dearly.
I want to hear you speak of Charlemagne.
He is so old, he's used up all his time—
from what I hear, he is past two hundred!
He has pushed his old body through so many lands,   525
taken so many blows on his buckled shield,
made beggars of so many mighty kings:
when will he lose the heart for making war?"
Ganelon answers: "Charles is not one to lose heart.
No man sees him, no man learns to know him   530
who does not say: the Emperor is great.
I do not know how to praise him so highly
that his great merit would not surpass my praise.
Who could recount his glory and his valor?
God put the light in him of such lordliness,   535
he would choose death before he failed his barons."

41.

Said the pagan: "I have reason to marvel
at Charlemagne, a man so old and gray—
he's two hundred years old, I hear, and more;
he has tortured his body through so many lands,   540
and borne so many blows from lance and spear,
made beggars of so many mighty kings:
when will he lose the heart for making war?"
"Never," said Ganelon, "while his nephew lives,
he's a fighter, there's no vassal like him   545
        under the vault of heaven. And he has friends.
There's Oliver, a good man, his companion.
And the Twelve Peers, whom Charles holds very dear,
form the vanguard, with twenty thousand knights.
Charles is secure, he fears no man on earth." AOI.

42.

Said the pagan: "Truly, how I must marvel   550
at Charlemagne, who is so gray and white—
over two hundred years, from what I hear;
gone through so many lands a conqueror,
and borne so many blows from strong sharp spears,
killed and conquered so many mighty kings: 555
when will he lose the heart for making war?"
"Never," said Ganelon, "while one man lives: Roland!
no man like him from here to the Orient!
There's his companion, Oliver, a brave man.
And the Twelve Peers, whom Charles holds very dear,   560
form the vanguard, with twenty thousand Franks.
Charles is secure, he fears no man alive." AOI.

43.

"Dear Lord Ganelon," said Marsilion the King,
"I have my army, you won't find one more handsome:
I can muster four hundred thousand knights!   565
With this host, now, can I fight Charles and the French?"
Ganelon answers: "No, no, don't try that now,
you'd take a loss: thousands of your pagans!
Forget such foolishness, listen to wisdom:
send the Emperor so many gifts   570
there'll be no Frenchman there who does not marvel.
For twenty hostages—those you'll be sending—
he will go home: home again to sweet France!
And he will leave his rear-guard behind him.
There will be Roland, I do believe, his nephew,   575
and Oliver, brave man, born to the court.
These Counts are dead, if anyone trusts me.
Then Charles will see that great pride of his go down,
he'll have no heart to make war on you again." AOI.

44.
"Dear Lord Ganelon," said Marsilion the King,   580
"What must I do to kill Roland the Count?"
Ganelon answers: "Now I can tell you that.
The King will be at Cize, in the great passes,
he will have placed his rear-guard at his back:
there'll be his nephew, Count Roland, that great man,   585
and Oliver, in whom he puts such faith,
and twenty thousand Franks in their company.
Now send one hundred thousand of your pagans
against the French—let them give the first battle.
The French army will be hit hard and shaken.   590
I must tell you: your men will be martyred.
Give them a second battle, then, like the first.
One will get him, Roland will not escape.
Then you'll have done a deed, a noble deed,
and no more war for the rest of your life!" AOI.   595

45.
"If someone can bring about the death of Roland,
then Charles would lose the right arm of his body,
that marvelous army would disappear—
never again could Charles gather such forces.
Then peace at last for the Land of Fathers!"   600
When Marsilion heard that, he kissed his neck.
Then he begins to open up his treasures. AOI.

46.
Marsilion said, "Why talk. . . .
No plan has any worth which one. . . .
Now swear to me that you will betray Roland."   605
Ganelon answers: "Let it be as you wish."
On the relics in his great sword Murgleis
he swore treason and became a criminal. AOI.

---

600. **The Land of Fathers:** *Tere Major,* in the text, can mean either "the great land,"
or "the land of fathers, ancestors." It always refers to France. See Joseph Bédier, *La
Chanson de Roland commentée* (Paris, 1927), p. 303.

603, 604: Parts of these lines are unintelligible in the manuscript.

47.

There stood a throne made all of ivory.
Marsilion commands them bring forth a book: 610
it was the law of Mahum and Tervagant.
This is the vow sworn by the Saracen of Spain:
if he shall find Roland in the rear-guard,
he shall fight him, all his men shall fight him,
and once he finds Roland, Roland will die.   615
Says Ganelon: "May it be as you will." AOI.

48.

And now there came a pagan, Valdabrun,
he was the man who raised Marsilion.
And, all bright smiles, he said to Ganelon:
"You take my sword, there's no man has one better: 620
a thousand coins, and more, are in the hilt.
It is a gift, dear lord, made in friendship,
only help us to Roland, that great baron,
let us find him standing in the rear-guard."
"It shall be done," replies Count Ganelon.   625
And then they kissed, on the face, on the chin.

49.

And there came then a pagan, Climborin,
and, all bright smiles, he said to Ganelon:
"You take my helmet, I never saw one better,
only help us to Roland, lord of the march,   630
show us the way to put Roland to shame."
"It shall be done," replied Count Ganelon.
And then they kissed, on the face, on the mouth. AOI.

50.

And then there came the Queen, Bramimunde;
said to the Count: "Lord, I love you well,   635
for my lord and all his men esteem you so.
I wish to send your wife two necklaces,
they are all gold, jacinths, and amethysts,
they are worth more than all the wealth of Rome.
Your Emperor has never seen their like."   640
He has taken them, thrusts them into his boot. AOI.

51.

The King calls for Malduit, his treasurer:
"The gifts for Charles—is everything prepared?"
And he replies: "Yes, Lord, and well prepared:
seven hundred camels, packed with gold and silver,   645
and twenty hostages, the noblest under heaven." AOI.

52.

Marsilion took Ganelon by the shoulder
and said to him: "You're a brave man, a wise man.
Now by that faith you think will save your soul,
take care you do not turn your heart from us.   650
I will give you a great mass of my wealth,
ten mules weighed down with fine Arabian gold;
and come each year, I'll do the same again.
Now you take these, the keys to this vast city:
present King Charles with all of its great treasure;   655
then get me Roland picked for the rear-guard.
Let me find him in some defile or pass,
I will fight him, a battle to the death."
Ganelon answers: "It's high time that I go."
Now he is mounted, and he is on his way. AOI.   660

53.

The Emperor moves homeward, he's drawing near.
Now he has reached the city of Valterne:
Roland had stormed it, destroyed it, and it stood
from that day forth a hundred years laid waste.
Charles is waiting for news of Ganelon   665
and the tribute from Spain, from that great land.
In the morning, at dawn, with the first light,
Count Ganelon came to the Christian camp. AOI.

54.

The Emperor rose early in the morning,
the King of France, and has heard mass and matins.   670
On the green grass he stood before his tent.
Roland was there, and Oliver, brave man,
Naimon the Duke, and many other knights.
Ganelon came, the traitor, the foresworn.
With what great cunning he commences his speech;   675
said to the King: "May the Lord God save you!
Here I bring you the keys to Saragossa.
And I bring you great treasure from that city,
and twenty hostages, have them well guarded.
And good King Marsilion sends you this word: 680
Do not blame him concerning the Algalife:
I saw it all myself, with my own eyes:
       four hundred thousand men, and all in arms,
their hauberks on, some with their helms laced on,
swords on their belts, the hilts enameled gold,
who went with him to the edge of the sea.   685
They are in flight: it is the Christian faith—
they do not want it, they will not keep its law.
They had not sailed four full leagues out to sea
when a high wind, a tempest swept them up.
They were all drowned; you will never see them;   690
if he were still alive, I'd have brought him.
As for the pagan King, Lord, believe this:
before you see one month from this day pass,
he'll follow you to the Kingdom of France
and take the faith—he will take your faith, Lord,   695
and join his hands and become your vassal.
He will hold Spain as a fief from your hand."
Then the King said: "May God be thanked for this.
You have done well, you will be well rewarded."
Throughout the host they sound a thousand trumpets.   700
The French break camp, strap their gear on their pack-horses.
They take the road to the sweet land of France. AOI.

55.

King Charlemagne laid waste the land of Spain,
stormed its castles, ravaged its citadels.
The King declares his war is at an end.   705
The Emperor rides toward the land of sweet France.
Roland the Count affixed the gonfanon,
raised it toward heaven on the height of a hill;
the men of France make camp across that country.
Pagans are riding up through these great valleys,   710
their hauberks on, their tunics of double mail,
their helms laced on, their swords fixed on their belts,
shields on their necks, lances trimmed with their banners.
In a forest high in the hills they gathered:
four hundred thousand men waiting for dawn.   715
God, the pity of it! the French do not know! AOI.

56.

The day goes by; now the darkness of night.
Charlemagne sleeps, the mighty Emperor.
He dreamt he was at Cize, in the great passes,
and in his fists held his great ashen lance.   720
Count Ganelon tore it away from him
and brandished it, shook it with such fury
the splinters of the shaft fly up toward heaven.
Charlemagne sleeps, his dream does not wake him.

57.

And after that he dreamed another vision: 725
he was in France, in his chapel at Aix,
a cruel wild boar was biting his right arm;
saw coming at him—from the Ardennes—a leopard,
it attacked him, fell wildly on his body.
And a swift hound running down from the hall   730
came galloping, bounding over to Charles,
tore the right ear off that first beast, the boar,
turns, in fury, to fight against the leopard.
And the French say: It is a mighty battle,
but cannot tell which one of them will win.   735
Charlemagne sleeps, his dream does not wake him. AOI.

58.

The day goes by, and the bright dawn arises.
Throughout that host. . . .
The Emperor rides forth with such fierce pride.
"Barons, my lords," said the Emperor Charles,   740
"look at those passes, at those narrow defiles—
pick me a man to command the rear-guard."
Ganelon answers: "Roland, here, my stepson.
You have no baron as great and brave as Roland."
When he hears that, the King stares at him in fury;   745
and said to him: "You are the living devil,
a mad dog—the murderous rage in you!
And who will precede me, in the vanguard?"
Ganelon answers, "Why, Ogier of Denmark,
you have no baron who could lead it so well."   750

59.

Roland the Count, when he heard himself named,
knew what to say, and spoke as a knight must speak:
"Lord Stepfather, I have to cherish you!
You have had the rear-guard assigned to me.
Charles will not lose, this great King who rules France,   755
I swear it now, one palfrey, one war horse—
      while I'm alive and know what's happening—
one he-mule, one she-mule that he might ride,
Charles will not lose one sumpter, not one pack horse
that has not first been bought and paid for with swords."
Ganelon answers: "You speak the truth, I know." AOI.   760

60.

When Roland hears he will lead the rear-guard,
he spoke in great fury to his stepfather:
"Hah! you nobody, you base-born little fellow,
and did you think the glove would fall from my hands
as the staff fell from yours before King Charles?" AOI.   765

738. Second hemistich unintelligible in the manuscript.

765. Ganelon had let fall a glove, not a staff (line 333). For this and other less objective reasons, some editors have questioned the authenticity of this *laisse*. In the following *laisse*, at line 769, a reviser tried to make the text more consistent by adding the reference to the staff.

61.

"Just Emperor," said Roland, that great man,
"give me the bow that you hold in your hand.
And no man here, I think, will say in reproach
I let it drop, as Ganelon let the staff drop
from his right hand, when he should have taken it."   770
The Emperor bowed down his head with this,
he pulled his beard, he twisted his mustache,
cannot hold back, tears fill his eyes, he weeps.

62.

And after that there came Naimon the Duke,
no greater vassal in the court than Naimon,   775
said to the King: "You've heard it clearly now:
it is Count Roland. How furious he is.
He is the one to whom the rear-guard falls,
no baron here can ever change that now.
Give him the bow that you have stretched and bent,   780
and then find him good men to stand with him."
The King gives him the bow; Roland has it now.

63.

The Emperor calls forth Roland the Count:
"My lord, my dear nephew, of course you know
I will give you half my men, they are yours.   785
Let them serve you, it is your salvation."
"None of that!" said the Count. "May God strike me
if I discredit the history of my line.
I'll keep twenty thousand Franks—they are good men.
Go your way through the passes, you will be safe.   790
You must not fear any man while I live."

64.

Roland the Count mounted his battle horse. AOI.
Oliver came to him, his companion.
And Gerin came, and the brave Count Gerer,
and Aton came, and there came Berenger,   .   795
and Astor came, and Anseïs, fierce and proud,
and the old man Gerard of Roussillon,
and Gaifier, that great and mighty duke.
Said the Archbishop: "I'm going, by my head!"
"And I with you," said Gautier the Count,   800
"I am Count Roland's man and must not fail him."
And together they choose twenty thousand men. AOI.

65.

Roland the Count summons Gautier de l'Hum:
"Now take a thousand Franks from our land, France,
and occupy those passes and the heights there.   805
The Emperor must not lose a single man." AOI.
Gautier replies: "Lord, I'll fight well for you."
And with a thousand French of France, their land,
Gautier rides out to the hills and defiles;
will not come down, for all the bad news, again,   810
till seven hundred swords have been drawn out.
King Almaris of the Kingdom of Belferne
gave them battle that day, and it was bitter.

66.

High are the hills, the valleys tenebrous,
the cliffs are dark, the defiles mysterious.   815
That day, and with much pain, the French passed through.
For fifteen leagues around one heard their clamor.
When they reach Tere Majur, the Land of Fathers,
they beheld Gascony, their lord's domain.
Then they remembered: their fiefs, their realms, their honors,   820
remembered their young girls, their gentle wives:
not one who does not weep for what he feels.
Beyond these others King Charles is in bad straits:
his nephew left in the defiles of Spain!
feels the pity of it; tears break through. AOI.   825

67.

And the Twelve Peers are left behind in Spain,
and twenty thousand Franks are left with them.
They have no fear, they have no dread of death.
The Emperor is going home to France.
Beneath his cloak, his face shows all he feels.   830
Naimon the Duke is riding beside him;
and he said to the King: "What is this grief?"
And Charles replies: "Whoever asks me, wrongs me.
I feel such pain, I cannot keep from wailing.
France will be destroyed by Ganelon.   835
Last night I saw a vision brought by angels:
the one who named my nephew for the rear-guard
shattered the lance between my fists to pieces.
I have left him in a march among strangers.
If I lose him, God! I won't find his like." AOI.   840

68.

King Charles the Great cannot keep from weeping.
A hundred thousand Franks feel pity for him;
and for Roland, an amazing fear.
Ganelon the criminal has betrayed him;
got gifts for it from the pagan king,   845
gold and silver, cloths of silk, gold brocade,
mules and horses and camels and lions.
Marsilion sends for the barons of Spain,
counts and viscounts and dukes and almaçurs,
and the emirs, and the sons of great lords: 850
four hundred thousand assembled in three days.
In Saragossa he has them beat the drums,
they raise Mahumet upon the highest tower:
no pagan now who does not worship him
and adore him. Then they ride, racing each other,   855
search through the land, the valleys, the mountains;
and then they saw the banners of the French.
The rear-guard of the Twelve Companions
will not fail now, they'll give the pagans battle.

69.

Marsilion's nephew has come forward   860
riding a mule that he goads with a stick;
said—a warrior's laugh on him—to his uncle:
"Dear Lord and King, how long I have served you,
and all the troubles, the pains I have endured,
so many battles fought and won on the field   865
Give me a fief, the first blow at Roland.
I will kill him, here's the spear I'll do it with.
If Mahumet will only stand by me,
I will set free every strip of land in Spain,
from the passes of Aspre to Durestant.   870
Charles will be weary, his Franks will give it up:
and no more war for the rest of your life!"
King Marsilion gave him his glove, as sign. AOI.

70.

The King's nephew holds the glove in his fist,
speaks these proud words to Marsilion his uncle: 875
"You've given me, dear Lord, King, a great gift!
Choose me twelve men, twelve of your noble barons,
and I will fight against the Twelve Companions."
And Falsaron was the first to respond—
he was the brother of King Marsilion: 880
"Dear Lord, Nephew, it's you and I together!
We'll fight, that's sure! We'll battle the rear-guard
of Charlemagne's grand army! We are the ones!
We have been chosen. We'll kill them all! It is fated." AOI.

71.

And now again: there comes King Corsablis,   885
a Berber, a bad man, a man of cunning;
and now he spoke as a brave vassal speaks:
for all God's gold he would not be a coward.
Now rushing up: Malprimis de Brigal,
faster on his two feet than any horse;   890
and cries great-voiced before Marsilion:
"I'm on my way to Rencesvals to fight!
Let me find Roland, I won't stop till I kill him!"

72.

There stands an amurafle, of Balaguer,
a fine figure, his face lit up with pride;   895
and when this man is mounted on his horse
and bears his arms, how fierce the look of him!
A great warrior, famed far and wide for fighting:
if he were Christian, he would be a great man.
Now he cried out before Marsilion: 900
"I'm on my way to Rencesvals to fight!
Let me find Roland and he is a dead man,
and Oliver, and all the Twelve Companions.
The French will die, in great pain, a vile death.
King Charles the Great is old, a child again;   905
he'll give it up, he'll lose heart for his war,
Spain will be ours at last, free and in peace."
Marsilion the King gave him great thanks. AOI.

894. **Amurafle:** emir.

73.

An almaçur of Moriane is there,
no worse scoundrel in all the land of Spain.   910
He made his boast before Marsilion:
"I am leading my people to Rencesvals,
twenty thousand good men with shields and lances.
Here's what I promise Roland: death, if I find him.
No day will pass that Charlemagne does not wail." AOI.   915

74.

And now again: Turgis of Turteluse:
he is a Count, and that city is his.
He wants to make his vow to slaughter Christians,
joins the others before Marsilion,
said to the King: "Never fear! Never fear!   920
Mahum is greater than Saint Peter of Rome!
Serve Mahum and the honor of the field is ours.
I'm off to Rencesvals to fight Roland,
and he will die, no man there can save him.
See my sword here, it is a good, long sword: 925
I'll put it up against his Durendal:
you will hear soon enough which one stayed up.
The French will die, if they dare come at us;
Charles, the old man—think of his pain and shame!
his head will wear no crown from that day on."   930

75.

And now again: Escremiz of Valterne:
a Saracen, and Valterne is his land;
stands in the crowd before Marsilion:
"I'll break that pride," he cries, "in Rencesvals!
Let me find Roland, he'll wear his head no more,   935
let me find Oliver, who leads the others.
The Twelve Peers are all most, they are marked men.
The French will die, France will lose its manhood,
and Charles will find no vassals in that wasteland." AOI.

---

909. **Almaçur:** "The Victorious," an honorific title.

76.

And now again: a pagan, Esturganz;   940
Estramariz, his companion, with him:
felons, liars, traitors, the both of them.
Said Marsilion: "You, my lords, come forward.
You are to go to the pass at Rencesvals.
The two of you will help to lead my army."   945
And they reply: "Lord, we are at your command.
We will attack Oliver and Roland;
no one can keep the Twelve Peers from their death.
These swords of ours are good, and they cut deep,
and we'll make them bright red with warm French blood.   950
How they will die, Charles will be wild with pain!
We'll put the Land of Fathers into your hands.
Come there, Lord, King, you will see it come true:
we'll make the Emperor beg you for mercy."

77.

Margariz of Seville came running up: 955
he holds the land down to the Cazmarines.
For his good looks ladies are friends of his—
not one sees him who does not light up toward him,
and seeing him she has to smile at him;
no pagan there can fight on horse like him;   960
crowds his way in, cries out above the others,
said to the King: "Never fear! Never fear!
I'm off to Rencesvals to kill Roland;
and Oliver will lay his life down there;
the Twelve Peers stand waiting for martyrdom.   965
Look at my sword, that's gold here in the hilt:
the Amiral of Primes sent me this gift.
I promise you, it will be bright with blood.
The French will die, France will be covered with shame.
Charles, that old man, with his flowering beard—   970
no day will dawn for him free of grief and rage.
Within one year we'll have France in our hands:
we'll sleep that night in the town of Saint-Denis!"
The pagan king bows to him profoundly. AOI.

967. **Amiral**: emir.

78.

And now again: Chernubles of Muneigre: 975
the hair on him sweeping down to the ground.
He lifts more weight, for fun, when he is joking,
than seven mules can bear all loaded down.
And of the land that he comes from they say
no sun shines there, and the grain cannot grow,   980
rain does not fall, and the dew does not gather,
there is no rock that is not black, all black;
and many say, devils live in that land.
Said Chernubles: "My good sword is on my belt,
I will stain it dark red in Rencesvals.   985
If I find Roland, that fighter, on my path,
and don't attack, then I'm not worth believing.
I'll conquer Durendal with this good sword,
the French will die, and their France will be crushed."
And with these words these twelve peers are assembled.   990
They take with them some hundred thousand pagans
who crowd forward, all rushing to do battle,
into a wood of pines, to arm themselves.

79.

They arm themselves in Saracen hauberks,
all but a few are lined with triple mail;   995
they lace on their good helms of Saragossa,
gird on their swords, the steel forged in Vienne;
they have rich shields, spears of Valencia,
and gonfanons of white and blue and red.
They leave the mules and riding horses now,   1000
mount their war horses and ride in close array.
The day was fair, the sun was shining bright,
all their armor was aflame with the light;
a thousand trumpets blow: that was to make it finer.
That made a great noise, and the men of France heard. 1005
Said Oliver: "Companion, I believe
we may yet have a battle with the pagans."
Roland replies: "Now may God grant us that.
We know our duty: to stand here for our King.
A man must bear some hardships for his lord,   1010
stand everything, the great heat, the great cold,
lose the hide and hair on him for his good lord.
Now let each man make sure to strike hard here:
let them not sing a bad song about us!
Pagans are wrong and Christians are right!   1015
They'll make no bad example of me this day!" AOI.

80.

Oliver climbs to the top of a hill,
looks to his right, across a grassy vale,
sees the pagan army on its way there;
and called down to Roland, his companion: 1020
"That way, toward Spain: the uproar I see coming!
All their hauberks, all blazing, helmets like flames!
It will be a bitter thing for our French.
Ganelon knew, that criminal, that traitor,
when he marked us out before the Emperor."   1025
"Be still, Oliver," Roland the Count replies.
"He is my stepfather—my stepfather.
        I won't have you speak one word against him."

81.

Oliver has gone up upon a hill,
sees clearly now: the kingdom of Spain,
and the Saracens assembled in such numbers: 1030
helmets blazing, bedecked with gems in gold,
those shields of theirs, those hauberks sewn with brass,
and all their spears, the gonfanons affixed;
cannot begin to count their battle corps,
there are too many, he cannot take their number.   1035
And he is deeply troubled by what he sees.
He made his way quickly down from the hill,
came to the French, told them all he had seen.

82.

Said Oliver: "I saw the Saracens,
no man on earth ever saw more of them—   1040
one hundred thousand, with their shields, up in front,
helmets laced on, hauberks blazing on them,
the shafts straight up, the iron heads like flames—
you'll get a battle, nothing like it before.
My lords, my French, may God give you the strength.   1045
Hold your ground now! Let them not defeat us!"
And the French say: "God hate the man who runs!
We may die here, but no man will fail you." AOI.

83.

Said Oliver: "The pagan force is great;
from what I see, our French here are too few.   1050
Roland, my companion, sound your horn then,
Charles will hear it, the army will come back."
Roland replies: "I'd be a fool to do it.
I would lose my good name all through sweet France.
I will strike now, I'll strike with Durendal,   1055
the blade will be bloody to the gold from striking!
These pagan traitors came to these passes doomed!
I promise you, they are marked men, they'll die." AOI.

84.

"Roland, Companion, now sound the olifant,
Charles will hear it, he will bring the army back,   1060
the King will come with all his barons to help us."
Roland replies: "May it never please God
that my kin should be shamed because of me,
or that sweet France should fall into disgrace.
Never! Never! I'll strike with Durendal,   1065
I'll strike with this good sword strapped to my side,
you'll see this blade running its whole length with blood.
These pagan traitors have gathered here to die.
I promise you, they are all bound for death." AOI.

85.

"Roland, Companion, sound your olifant now,   1070
Charles will hear it, marching through those passes.
I promise you, the Franks will come at once."
Roland replies: "May it never please God
that any man alive should come to say
that pagans—pagans!—once made me sound this horn: 1075
no kin of mine will ever bear that shame.
Once I enter this great battle coming
and strike my thousand seven hundred blows,
you'll see the bloody steel of Durendal.
These French are good—they will strike like brave men.   1080
Nothing can save the men of Spain from death."

86.

Said Oliver: "I see no blame in it—
I watched the Saracens coming from Spain,
the valleys and mountains covered with them,
every hillside and every plain all covered,   1085
hosts and hosts everywhere of those strange men—
and here we have a little company."
Roland replies: "That whets my appetite.
May it not please God and his angels and saints
to let France lose its glory because of me—   1090
let me not end in shame, let me die first.
The Emperor loves us when we fight well."

87.

Roland is good, and Oliver is wise,
both these vassals men of amazing courage:
once they are armed and mounted on their horses,   1095
they will not run, though they die for it, from battle.
Good men, these Counts, and their words full of spirit.
Traitor pagans are riding up in fury.
Said Oliver: "Roland, look—the first ones,
on top of us—and Charles is far away.   1100
You did not think it right to sound your olifant:
if the King were here, we'd come out without losses.
Now look up there, toward the passes of Aspre—
you can see the rear-guard: it will suffer.
No man in that detail will be in another."   1105
Roland replies: "Don't speak such foolishness—
shame on the heart gone coward in the chest.
We'll hold our ground, we'll stand firm—we're the ones!
We'll fight with spears, we'll fight them hand to hand!" AOI.

88.

When Roland sees that there will be a battle,   1110
it makes him fiercer than a lion or leopard;
shouts to the French, calls out to Oliver:
"Lord, companion: friend, do not say such things.
The Emperor, who left us these good French,
had set apart these twenty thousand men: 1115
he knew there was no coward in their ranks.
A man must meet great troubles for his lord,
stand up to the great heat and the great cold,
give up some flesh and blood—it is his duty.
Strike with the lance, I'll strike with Durendal—   1120
it was the King who gave me this good sword!
If I die here, the man who gets it can say:
it was a noble's, a vassal's, a good man's sword."

89.

And now there comes the Archbishop Turpin.
He spurs his horse, goes up into a mountain,   1125
summons the French; and he preached them a sermon:
"Barons, my lords, Charles left us in this place.
We know our duty: to die like good men for our King.
Fight to defend the holy Christian faith.
Now you will have a battle, you know it now,   1130
you see the Saracens with your own eyes.
Confess your sins, pray to the Lord for mercy.
I will absolve you all, to save your souls.
If you die here, you will stand up holy martyrs,
you will have seats in highest Paradise."   1135
The French dismount, cast themselves on the ground;
the Archbishop blesses them in God's name.
He commands them to do one penance: strike.

90.

The French arise, stand on their feet again;
they are absolved, released from all their sins: 1140
the Archbishop has blessed them in God's name.
Now they are mounted on their swift battle horses,
bearing their arms like faithful warriors;
and every man stands ready for the battle.
Roland the Count calls out to Oliver: 1145
"Lord, Companion, you knew it, you were right,
Ganelon watched for his chance to betray us,
got gold for it, got goods for it, and money.
The Emperor will have to avenge us now.
King Marsilion made a bargain for our lives,   1150
but still must pay, and that must be with swords." AOI.

91.

Roland went forth into the Spanish passes
on Veillantif, his good swift-running horse.
He bears his arms—how they become this man!—
grips his lance now, hefting it, working it,   1155
now swings the iron point up toward the sky,
the gonfanon all white laced on above—
the golden streamers beat down upon his hands:
a noble's body, the face aglow and smiling.
Close behind him his good companion follows;   1160
the men of France hail him: their protector!
He looks wildly toward the Saracens,
and humbly and gently to the men of France;
and spoke a word to them, in all courtesy:
"Barons, my lords, easy now, keep at a walk.   1165
These pagans are searching for martyrdom.
We'll get good spoils before this day is over,
no king of France ever got such treasure!"
And with these words, the hosts are at each other. AOI.

92.

Said Oliver: "I will waste no more words.   1170
You did not think it right to sound your olifant,
there'll be no Charles coming to your aid now.
He knows nothing, brave man, he's done no wrong;
those men down there—they have no blame in this.
Well, then, ride now, and ride with all your might!   1175
Lords, you brave men, stand your ground, hold the field!
Make up your minds, I beg you in God's name,
to strike some blows, take them and give them back!
Here we must not forget Charlemagne's war cry."
And with that word the men of France cried out.   1180
A man who heard that shout: Munjoie! Munjoie!
would always remember what manhood is.
Then they ride, God! look at their pride and spirit!
and they spur hard, to ride with all their speed,
come on to strike—what else would these men do?   1185
The Saracens kept coming, never fearing them.
Franks and pagans, here they are, at each other.

93.

Marsilion's nephew is named Aëlroth.
He rides in front, at the head of the army,
comes on shouting insults against our French: 1190
"French criminals, today you fight our men.
One man should have saved you: he betrayed you.
A fool, your King, to leave you in these passes.
This is the day sweet France will lose its name,
and Charlemagne the right arm of his body."   1195
When he hears that—God!—Roland is outraged!
He spurs his horse, gives Veillantif its head.
The Count comes on to strike with all his might,
smashes his shield, breaks his hauberk apart,
and drives: rips through his chest, shatters the bones,   1200
knocks the whole backbone out of his back,
casts out the soul of Aëlroth with his lance;
which he thrusts deep, makes the whole body shake,
throws him down dead, lance straight out, from his horse;
he has broken his neck; broken it in two.   1205
There is something, he says, he must tell him:
"Clown! Nobody! Now you know Charles is no fool,
he never was the man to love treason.
It took his valor to leave us in these passes!
France will not lose its name, sweet France! today.   1210
Brave men of France, strike hard! The first blow is ours!
We're in the right, and these swine in the wrong!" AOI.

1204. **Lance straight out** (*pleine sa hanste*, "with his full lance"): the lance is held,
not thrown, and used to knock the enemy from his horse. To throw one's weapons is
savage and ignoble. Note *laisses* 154 and 160, and the outlandish names of the things
the pagans throw at Roland, Gautier, and Turpin.

94.

A duke is there whose name is Falsaron,
he was the brother of King Marsilion,
held the wild land of Dathan and Abiram;   1215
under heaven, no criminal more vile;
a tremendous forehead between his eyes—
a good half-foot long, if you had measured it.
His pain is bitter to see his nephew dead;
rides out alone, baits the foe with his body,   1220
and riding shouts the war cry of the pagans,
full of hate and insults against the French:
"This is the day sweet France will lose its honor!"
Oliver hears, and it fills him with fury,
digs with his golden spurs into his horse,   1225
comes on to strike the blow a baron strikes,
smashes his shield, breaks his hauberk apart,
thrusts into him the long streamers of his gonfalon,
knocks him down, dead, lance straight out, from the saddle;
looks to the ground and sees the swine stretched out,   1230
and spoke these words—proud words, terrible words:
"You nobody, what are your threats to me!
Men of France, strike! Strike and we will beat them!"
Munjoie! he shouts—the war cry of King Charles. AOI.

1215. **Dathan and Abiram:** See Numbers, 16:1–35

95.

A king is there whose name is Corsablis,   1235
a Berber, come from that far country.
He spoke these words to all his Saracens:
"Now here's one battle we'll have no trouble with,
look at that little troop of Frenchmen there,
a few odd men—they're not worth noticing!   1240
King Charles won't save a single one of them.
Their day has come, they must all die today."
And Archbishop Turpin heard every word:
no man on earth he wants so much to hate!
digs with spurs of fine gold into his horse,   1245
comes on to strike with all his awful might;
smashed through his shield, burst the rings of his hauberk,
sent his great lance into the body's center,
drove it in deep, he made the dead man shake,
knocked him down, dead, lance straight out, on the road;   1250
looks to the ground and sees the swine stretched out;
there is something, he says, he must tell him:
"You pagan! You nobody! You told lies there:
King Charles my lord is our safeguard forever!
Our men of France have no heart for running.   1255
As for your companions—we'll nail them to the ground;
and then you must all die the second death.
At them, you French! No man forget what he is!
Thanks be to God, now the first blow is ours";
and shouts Munjoie! Munjoie! to hold the field.   1260

96.

And Gerin strikes Malprimis of Brigal,
who finds his good shield now not worth one cent;
shatters the precious boss of pure crystal,
knocks the whole half of it down to the ground;
bursts through the hauberk's rings into the flesh,   1265
buries his good lance deep in his body;
the pagan falls, all his sinews one mass,
down to the ground. Satan takes away his soul. AOI.

97.

And Gerer, his companion, strikes the Amurafle,
rips through his shield, the rings of his hauberk,   1270
sends his good lance tearing through his entrails,
drives it in well, it passes through his body,
knocks him down, dead, lance straight out, on the ground.
Said Oliver: "We're fighting like good men."

1257. **The second death:** the death of the soul, eternal damnation. See Revelation,
20:11–15; 21:8.

98.

Samson the Duke! strikes the Almaçur,   1275
smashes his shield adorned with gold and flowers,
that good hauberk cannot protect him now;
cuts through the heart, the liver, the lung,
knocks him down dead; that may grieve some: not others!
Said the Archbishop: "That's how a baron strikes!"   1280

99.

And Anseïs gives his war horse its head,
comes on to strike Turgis of Turteluse;
smashes his shield under the golden boss
and breaks apart his hauberk's double rings;
sends the good lance's head ripping through his body,   1285
drives it in well, gets all the iron through,
knocks him back, lance straight out, dead on the field.
And Roland said: "That's how a good man strikes!"

100.

And Engeler, the Gascon, of Bordeaux,
spurs on his battle horse, gives him the reins,   1290
comes on to strike Escremiz of Valterne;
smashes the shield to pieces on his neck,
bursts the hood's rings of his hauberk apart,
strikes between the two forks, square in the chest,
knocks him down, dead, lance straight out, from the saddle;   1295
then said to him: "On your way to perdition!" AOI.

101.

And Aton strikes the pagan Estorgant,
comes through his shield down from the upper edge
straight through, and cuts away the red and white;
and broke apart the panels of his hauberk,   1300
sends his good lance tearing into his body,
knocks him down, dead, from his swift-running horse;
then said to him: "Go now, find your protector!"

102.

And Berenger! strikes Estramariz,
smashes his shield, bursts the rings of his hauberk,   1305
sends his strong spear tearing into his middle,
knocks him down, dead, among a thousand pagan dead.
Of these twelve pagan peers ten have been killed,
there are but two still alive on that field:
these are Chernuble and Margariz the Count.   1310

1294. **Between the two forks:** between the collar bone and the hollow above the belly.

103.

Margariz is a fighter, and very brave,
handsome and strong, quick in his moves, adroit;
spurs his war horse: he will strike Oliver;
smashes his shield under the boss of fine gold,
drove in his spear, it passed along his side: 1315
God protects him: it never touched his body;
the long shaft breaks, he could not bring him down.
Away rides Margariz, his way is clear,
and sounds his horn to rally all his men.

104.

The battle is fearful and wonderful   1320
and everywhere. Roland never spares himself,
strikes with his lance as long as the wood lasts:
the fifteenth blow he struck, it broke, was lost.
Then he draws Durendal, his good sword, bare,
and spurs his horse, comes on to strike Chernuble,   1325
smashes his helmet, carbuncles shed their light,
cuts through the coif, through the hair on his head,
cut through his eyes, through his face, through that look,
the bright, shining hauberk with its fine rings,
down through the trunk to the fork of his legs,   1330
through the saddle, adorned with beaten gold,
into the horse; and the sword came to rest:
cut through the spine, never felt for the joint;
knocks him down, dead, on the rich grass of the meadow;
then said to him: "You were doomed when you started,   1336
Clown! Nobody! Let Mahum help you now.
No pagan swine will win this field today."

1319. And so Margariz, beloved of women (see *laisse* 77), rides out of the poem, not
to be heard from again. He was probably meant to be the one who informs Marsilion
about the destruction of the first army—a scene that appears in the version that is clos-
est to the Oxford *Roland* (MS. V4, *laisses* 111 and 112). See Bédier, *La Chanson de
Roland commentée*, pp. 182–88.

105.

Roland the Count comes riding through the field,
holds Durendal, that sword! it carves its way!
and brings terrible slaughter down on the pagans.   1340
To have seen him cast one man dead on another,
the bright red blood pouring out on the ground,
his hauberk, his two arms, running with blood,
his good horse—neck and shoulders running with blood!
And Oliver does not linger, he strikes!   1345
and the Twelve Peers, no man could reproach them;
and the brave French, they fight with lance and sword.
The pagans die, some simply faint away!
Said the Archbishop: "Bless our band of brave men!"
Munjoie! he shouts—the war cry of King Charles. AOI.   1350

106.

Oliver rides into that battle-storm,
his lance is broken, he holds only the stump;
comes on to strike a pagan, Malsarun;
and he smashes his shield, all flowers and gold,
sends his two eyes flying out of his head,   1355
and his brains come pouring down to his feet;
casts him down, dead, with seven hundred others.
Now he has killed Turgis and Esturguz,
and the shaft bursts, shivers down to his fists.
Count Roland said: "Companion, what are you doing?   1360
Why bother with a stick in such a battle?
Iron and steel will do much better work!
Where is your sword, your Halteclere—that name!
Where is that crystal hilt, that golden guard?"
"Haven't had any time to draw it out,   1365
been so busy fighting," said Oliver. AOI.

107.

Lord Oliver has drawn out his good sword—
that sword his companion had longed to see—
and showed him how a good man uses it:
strikes a pagan, Justin of Val Ferrée,   1370
and comes down through his head, cuts through the center,
through his body, his hauberk sewn with brass,
the good saddle beset with gems in gold,
into the horse, the backbone cut in two;
knocks him down, dead, before him on the meadow.   1375
Count Roland said: "Now I know it's you, Brother.
The Emperor loves us for blows like that."
Munjoie! that cry! goes up on every side. AOI.

108.

Gerin the Count sits on his bay Sorél
and Gerer his companion on Passe-Cerf;   1380
and they ride, spurring hard, let loose their reins,
come on to strike a pagan, Timozel,
one on his shield, the other on his hauberk.
They broke their two lances in his body;
turn him over, dead, in a fallow field.   1385
I do not know and have never heard tell
which of these two was swifter, though both were swift.
Esperveris: he was the son of Borel
and now struck dead by Engeler of Bordeaux.
Turpin the Archbishop killed Siglorel,   1390
the enchanter, who had been in Hell before:
Jupiter brought him there, with that strange magic.
Then Turpin said: "That swine owed us his life!"
Roland replies: "And now the scoundrel's dead.
Oliver, Brother, those were blows! I approve!"   1395

109.

In the meantime, the fighting grew bitter.
Franks and pagans, the fearful blows they strike—
those who attack, those who defend themselves;
so many lances broken, running with blood,
the gonfanons in shreds, the ensigns torn,   1400
so many good French fallen, their young lives lost:
they will not see their mothers or wives again,
or the men of France who wait for them at the passes. AOI.
Charlemagne waits and weeps and wails for them.
What does that matter? They'll get no help from him.   1405
Ganelon served him ill that day he sold,
in Saragossa, the barons of his house.
He lost his life and limbs for what he did:
was doomed to hang in the great trial at Aix,
and thirty of his kin were doomed with him,   1410
who never expected to die that death. AOI.

110.

The battle is fearful and full of grief.
Oliver and Roland strike like good men,
the Archbishop, more than a thousand blows,
and the Twelve Peers do not hang back, they strike!   1415
the French fight side by side, all as one man.
The pagans die by hundreds, by thousands: .
whoever does not flee finds no refuge from death,
like it or not, there he ends all his days.
And there the men of France lose their greatest arms;   1420
they will not see their fathers, their kin again,
or Charlemagne, who looks for them in the passes.
Tremendous torment now comes forth in France,
a mighty whirlwind, tempests of wind and thunder,
rains and hailstones, great and immeasurable,   1425
bolts of lightning hurtling and hurtling down:
it is, in truth, a trembling of the earth.
From Saint Michael-in-Peril to the Saints,
from Besançon to the port of Wissant,
there is no house whose veil of walls does not crumble.   1430
A great darkness at noon falls on the land,
there is no light but when the heavens crack.
No man sees this who is not terrified,
and many say: "The Last Day! Judgment Day!
The end! The end of the world is upon us!"   1435
They do not know, they do not speak the truth:
it is the worldwide grief for the death of Roland.

111.

The French have fought with all their hearts and strength,
pagans are dead by the thousands, in droves:
of one hundred thousand, not two are saved.   1440
Said the Archbishop: "Our men! What valiant fighters!
No king under heaven could have better.
It is written in the Gesta Francorum:
our Emperor's vassals were all good men."
They walk over the field to seek their dead,   1445
they weep, tears fill their eyes, in grief and pity
for their kindred, with love, with all their hearts.
Marsilion the King, with all his men
        in that great host, rises up before them. AOI.

1428–29: Although the designation *Seinz* ("Saints") is uncertain (it may refer, according to various proposals, to Cologne, to Xanten on the lower Rhine, or to Sens, in Burgundy), it is clear that these four points mark out the France of the tenth century, the realm of the last Carolingians. See R. Louis, "La grande douleur pour la mort de Roland," *Cahiers de Civilisation Médiévale*, 3 (1960), 62–67; summarized in the *Bulletin bibliographique de la Société Rencesvals*, 2 (1960), 73–76.

112.

King Marsilion comes along a valley
with all his men, the great host he assembled: 1450
twenty divisions, formed and numbered by the King,
helmets ablaze with gems beset in gold,
and those bright shields, those hauberks sewn with brass.
Seven thousand clarions sound the pursuit,
and the great noise resounds across that country. 1455
Said Roland then: "Oliver, Companion, Brother,
that traitor Ganelon has sworn our deaths:
it is treason, it cannot stay hidden,
the Emperor will take his terrible revenge.
We have this battle now, it will be bitter, 1460
no man has ever seen the like of it.
I will fight here with Durendal, this sword,
and you, my companion, with Halteclere—
we've fought with them before, in many lands!
how many battles have we won with these two! 1465
Let no one sing a bad song of our swords." AOI.

115.   [113]*

When the French see the pagans so numerous, 1510
the fields swarming with them on every side,
they call the names of Oliver, and Roland,
and the Twelve Peers: protect them, be their warranter. [1470]
The Archbishop told them how he saw things:
"Barons, my lords, do not think shameful thoughts, 1515
do not, I beg you all in God's name, run.
Let no brave man sing shameful songs of us:
let us all die here fighting: that is far better. [1475]
We are promised: we shall soon find our deaths,
after today we won't be living here. 1520
But here's one thing, and I am your witness:
Holy Paradise lies open to you,
you will take seats among the Innocents." [1480]
And with these words the Franks are filled with joy,
there is no man who does not shout Munjoie! AOI. 1525

* Laisses 113–26 as they appear in the manuscript are obviously out of order. The present sequence is that followed by most editors, including Segre. The number without brackets indicates the original place of each laisse and each line in the manuscript; the number in brackets follows the revised order.

116. [114]

A Saracen was there of Saragossa,
half that city was in this pagan's keeping,
this Climborin, who fled before no man,   [1485]
who took the word of Ganelon the Count,
kissed in friendship the mouth that spoke that word,   1530
gave him a gift: his helmet and its carbuncle.
Now he will shame, says he, the Land of Fathers,
he will tear off the crown of the Emperor;   [1490]
sits on the horse that he calls Barbamusche,
swifter than the sparrowhawk, than the swallow;   1535
digs in his spurs, gives that war horse its head,
comes on to strike Engeler of Gascony,
whose shield and fine hauberk cannot save him;   [1495]
gets the head of his spear into his body,
drives it in deep, gets all the iron through,   1540
throws him back, dead, lance straight out, on the field.
And then he cries: "It's good to kill these swine!
At them, Pagans! At them and break their ranks!"   [1500]
"God!" say the French, "the loss of that good man!" AOI.

117. [115]

Roland the Count calls out to Oliver: 1545
"Lord, Companion, there is Engeler dead,
we never had a braver man on horse."
The Count replies: "God let me avenge him";   [1505]
and digs with golden spurs into his horse,
grips—the steel running with blood—Halteclere,   1550
comes on to strike with all his mighty power:
the blow comes flashing down; the pagan falls.
Devils take away the soul of Climborin.   [1510]
And then he killed Alphaïen the duke,
cut off the head of Escababi,   1555
struck from their horses seven great Arrabites:
they'll be no use for fighting any more!
And Roland said: "My companion is enraged!   [1515]
Why, he compares with me! he earns his praise!
Fighting like that makes us dearer to Charles";   1560
lifts up his voice and shouts: "Strike! you are warriors!" AOI.

118.   [116]
And now again: a pagan, Valdabrun,
the man who raised Marsilion from the font,   [1520]
lord of four hundred dromonds that sail the sea:
there is no sailor who does not call him lord;   1565
the man who took Jerusalem by treason:
he violated the temple of Solomon,
he killed the Patriarch before the fonts;   [1525]
took the sworn word of Ganelon the Count,
gave him his sword and a thousand gold coins.   1570
He rides the horse that he calls Gramimund,
swifter by far than the falcon that flies;
digs hard into its flanks with his sharp spurs,   [1530]
comes on to strike Sansun, our mighty duke:
smashes his shield, bursts the rings of his hauberk,   1575
drives in the streamers of his bright gonfanon,
knocks him down, dead, lance straight out, from the saddle:
"Saracens, strike! Strike and we will beat them."   [1535]
"God!" say the French, "the loss of that great man!" AOI.

119.   [117]
Roland the Count, when he sees Sansun dead—   1580
now, lords, you know the rage, the pain he felt;
digs in his spurs, runs at that man in fury,
grips Durendal, more precious than fine gold,   [1540]
comes on, brave man, to strike with all his power
on his helmet, beset with gems in gold,   1585
cuts through the head, the hauberk, the strong body,
the good saddle beset with gems in gold,
into the back, profoundly, of the horse,   [1545]
and kills them both, praise him or damn him who will.
Say the pagans: "A terrible blow for us!"   1590
Roland replies: "I cannot love your men,
all the wrong and presumption are on your side." AOI.

120.   [118.]
An African, come there from Africa,   [1550]
is Malquidant, the son of King Malcud,
his battle gear studded with beaten gold: 1595
he shines to heaven, aflame among the others,
rides the war horse that he calls Salt Perdut—
no beast on earth could ever run with him;   [1555]
comes on to strike Anseïs, strikes on his shield
straight down, and cut away the red and blue,   1600
burst into shreds the panels of his hauberk,
thrust into him the iron and the shaft.
The Count is dead, his days are at an end.   [1560]
And the French say: "Lord, you fought well and died!"

121.   [119.]

Across the field rides Archbishop Turpin.   1605
Tonsured singer of masses! Where is the priest
who drove his body to do such mighty deeds?
said to the pagan: "God send you every plague,   [1565]
you killed a man it pains my heart to remember";
and sent his good war horse charging ahead,   1610
struck on that pagan shield of Toledo;
and he casts him down, dead, on the green grass.

122.   [120.]

And now again: a pagan, Grandonie,   [1570]
son of Capuel, the king of Cappadocia;
he is mounted on the horse he calls Marmorie,   1615
swifter by far than the bird on the wing;
loosens the reins, digs in sharp with his spurs,
comes on to strike with his great strength Gerin, [1575]
shatters the dark red shield, drags it from his neck,
and driving bursts the meshes of his hauberk,   1620
thrusts into him the blue length of his banner
and casts him down, dead, upon a high rock;
and goes on, kills Gerer, his dear companion,   [1580]
and Berenger, and Guion of Saint Antonie;
goes on still, strikes Austorie, a mighty duke   1625
who held Valence and Envers on the Rhone;
knocks him down, dead, puts joy into the pagans.
The French cry out: "Our men are losing strength!" [1585]

123.   [121.]

Count Roland holds his sword running with blood;
he has heard them: men of France losing heart;   1630
filled with such pain, he feels he will break apart;
said to the pagan: "God send you every plague,
the man you killed, I swear, will cost you dear";   [1590]
his war horse, spurred, runs straining every nerve.
One must pay, they have come face to face.   1635

124.   [122.]

Grandonie was a great and valiant man,
and very strong, a fighter; and in his path
he came on Roland, had never seen him before;   [1595]
but knew him now, knew him now, knew him now,
that fury on his face, that lordly body,   1640
that look, and that look, the tremendous sight of him;
does not know how to keep down his panic,
and wants to run, but that will not save him;   [1600]
the blow comes down, Roland's strength is in it,
splits his helmet through the nosepiece in two,   1645
cuts through the nose, through the mouth, through the teeth,
down through the trunk, the Algerian mail,
the silver bows of that golden saddle,   [1605]
into the back, profoundly, of the horse;
and killed them both, they never rode again.   1650
The men of Spain cry out their rage and grief.
And the French say: "Our defender has struck!"

126.   [123.]

The battle is fearful, there is no rest,   [1610]
and the French strike with all their rage and strength,
cut through their fists and their sides and their spines,
cut through their garments into the living flesh,
the bright blood flows in streams on the green grass.   1665
The pagans cry: "We can't stand up to this!   [1615]
Land of Fathers, Mahummet's curse on you!
Your men are hard, we never saw such men!"
There is not one who does not cry: "Marsilion!
Come to us, King! Ride! We are in need! Help!"   1670

125.   [124.]

The battle is fearful, and vast,   [1620]
the men of France strike hard with burnished lances.
There you would have seen the great pain of warriors,   1655
so many men dead and wounded and bleeding,
one lies face up, face down, on another.
The Saracens cannot endure it longer.   [1625]
Willing and unwilling they quit the field.
The French pursue, with all their heart and strength. AOI.   1660

Laisse 125. Segre numbers this laisse 124[b] [122[b]]. From here on, each *laisse* in the
translation will be one number higher than the corresponding *laisse* in the text.

113.   [125.]
Marsilion sees his people's martyrdom.
He commands them: sound his horns and trumpets;
and he rides now with the great host he has gathered.   [1630]
At their head rides the Saracen Abisme: 1470
no worse criminal rides in that company,
stained with the marks of his crimes and great treasons,
lacking the faith in God, Saint Mary's son.
And he is black, as black as melted pitch,   [1635]
a man who loves murder and treason more   1475
than all the gold of rich Galicia,
no living man ever saw him play or laugh;
a great fighter, a wild man, mad with pride,
and therefore dear to that criminal king;   [1640]
holds high his dragon, where all his people gather.   1480
The Archbishop will never love that man,
no sooner saw than wanted to strike him;
considered quietly, said to himself:
"That Saracen—a heretic, I'll wager.   [1645]
Now let me die if I do not kill him—   1485
I never loved cowards or cowards' ways." AOI.

114.   [126.]
Turpin the Archbishop begins the battle.
He rides the horse that he took from Grossaille,
who was a king this priest once killed in Denmark.   [1650]
Now this war horse is quick and spirited,   1490
his hooves high-arched, the quick legs long and flat,
short in the thigh, wide in the rump, long in the flanks,
and the backbone so high, a battle horse!
and that white tail, the yellow mane on him,   [1655]
the little ears on him, the tawny head!   1495
No beast on earth could ever run with him.
The Archbishop—that valiant man!—spurs hard,
he will attack Abisme, he will not falter,
strikes on his shield, a miraculous blow: [1660]
a shield of stones, of amethysts, topazes,   1500
esterminals, carbuncles all on fire—
a gift from a devil, in Val Metas,
sent on to him by the Amiral Galafre.
There Turpin strikes, he does not treat it gently—   [1665]
after that blow, I'd not give one cent for it;   1505
cut through his body, from one side to the other,
and casts him down dead in a barren place.
And the French say: "A fighter, that Archbishop!
Look at him there, saving souls with that crozier!"   [1670]

127.

Roland the Count calls out to Oliver:
"Lord, Companion, now you have to agree
the Archbishop is a good man on horse,
there's none better on earth or under heaven,
he knows his way with a lance and a spear."   1675
The Count replies: "Right! Let us help him then."
And with these words the Franks began anew,
the blows strike hard, and the fighting is bitter;
there is a painful loss of Christian men.
To have seen them, Roland and Oliver,   1680
these fighting men, striking down with their swords,
the Archbishop with them, striking with his lance!
One can recount the number these three killed:
it is written—in charters, in documents;
the Geste tells it: it was more than four thousand.   1685
Through four assaults all went well with our men;
then comes the fifth, and that one crushes them.
They are all killed, all these warriors of France,
all but sixty, whom the Lord God has spared:
they will die too, but first sell themselves dear. AOI.   1690

128.

Count Roland sees the great loss of his men,
calls on his companion, on Oliver:
"Lord, Companion, in God's name, what would you do?
All these good men you see stretched on the ground.
We can mourn for sweet France, fair land of France!   1695
a desert now, stripped of such great vassals.
Oh King, and friend, if only you were here!
Oliver, Brother, how shall we manage it?
What shall we do to get word to the King?"
Said Oliver: "I don't see any way.   1700
I would rather die now than hear us shamed." AOI.

129.

And Roland said: "I'll sound the olifant,
Charles will hear it, drawing through the passes,
I promise you, the Franks will return at once."
Said Oliver: "That would be a great disgrace,   1705
a dishonor and reproach to all your kin,
the shame of it would last them all their lives.
When I urged it, you would not hear of it;
you will not do it now with my consent.
It is not acting bravely to sound it now—   1710
look at your arms, they are covered with blood."
The Count replies: "I've fought here like a lord." AOI.

130.

And Roland says: "We are in a rough battle.
I'll sound the olifant, Charles will hear it."
Said Oliver: "No good vassal would do it.   1715
When I urged it, friend, you did not think it right.
If Charles were here, we'd come out with no losses.
Those men down there—no blame can fall on them."
Oliver said: "Now by this beard of mine,
If I can see my noble sister, Aude,   1720
once more, you will never lie in her arms!" AOI.

131.

And Roland said: "Why are you angry at me?"
Oliver answers: "Companion, it is your doing.
I will tell you what makes a vassal good:
     it is judgment, it is never madness;
restraint is worth more than the raw nerve of a fool.   1725
Frenchmen are dead because of your wildness.
And what service will Charles ever have from us?
If you had trusted me, my lord would be here,
we would have fought this battle through to the end,
Marsilion would be dead, or our prisoner.   1730
Roland, your prowess—had we never seen it!
     And now, dear friend, we've seen the last of it.
No more aid from us now for Charlemagne,
a man without equal till Judgment Day,
you will die here, and your death will shame France.
We kept faith, you and I, we were companions;   1735
     and everything we were will end today.
We part before evening, and it will be hard." AOI.

1710–12. Some have found these lines difficult. Oliver means: We have fought this
far—look at the enemy's blood on your arms: It is too late, it would be a disgrace to
summon help when there is no longer any chance of being saved. And Roland thinks
that that is the one time when it is not a disgrace.

132.

Turpin the Archbishop hears their bitter words,
digs hard into his horse with golden spurs
and rides to them; begins to set them right:
"You, Lord Roland, and you, Lord Oliver,   1740
I beg you in God's name do not quarrel.
To sound the horn could not help us now, true,
but still it is far better that you do it:
let the King come, he can avenge us then—
these men of Spain must not go home exulting!   1745
Our French will come, they'll get down on their feet,
and find us here—we'll be dead, cut to pieces.
They will lift us into coffins on the backs of mules,
and weep for us, in rage and pain and grief,
and bury us in the courts of churches;   1750
and we will not be eaten by wolves or pigs or dogs."
Roland replies, "Lord, you have spoken well." AOI.

133.

Roland has put the olifant to his mouth,
he sets it well, sounds it with all his strength.
The hills are high, and that voice ranges far,   1755
they heard it echo thirty great leagues away.
King Charles heard it, and all his faithful men.
And the King says: "Our men are in a battle."
And Ganelon disputed him and said:
"Had someone else said that, I'd call him liar!" AOI.   1760

134.

And now the mighty effort of Roland the Count:
he sounds his olifant; his pain is great,
and from his mouth the bright blood comes leaping out,
and the temple bursts in his forehead.
That horn, in Roland's hands, has a mighty voice: 1765
King Charles hears it drawing through the passes.
Naimon heard it, the Franks listen to it.
And the King said: "I hear Count Roland's horn;
he'd never sound it unless he had a battle."
Says Ganelon: "Now no more talk of battles!   1770
You are old now, your hair is white as snow,
the things you say make you sound like a child.
You know Roland and that wild pride of his—   *deceit*
what a wonder God has suffered it so long!
Remember? he took Noples without your command: 1775
the Saracens rode out, to break the siege;
they fought with him, the great vassal Roland.
Afterwards he used the streams to wash the blood
from the meadows: so that nothing would show.
He blasts his horn all day to catch a rabbit,   1780
he's strutting now before his peers and bragging—
who under heaven would dare meet him on the field?
So now: ride on! Why do you keep on stopping?
The Land of Fathers lies far ahead of us." AOI.

135.

The blood leaping from Count Roland's mouth,   1785
the temple broken with effort in his forehead,
he sounds his horn in great travail and pain.
King Charles heard it, and his French listen hard.
And the King said: "That horn has a long breath!"
Naimon answers: "It is a baron's breath.   1790
There is a battle there, I know there is.
He betrayed him! and now asks you to fail him!
Put on your armor! Lord, shout your battle cry,
and save the noble barons of your house!
You hear Roland's call. He is in trouble."   1795

136.

The Emperor commanded the horns to sound,
the French dismount, and they put on their armor:
their hauberks, their helmets, their gold-dressed swords,
their handsome shields; and take up their great lances,
the gonfalons of white and red and blue.   1800
The barons of that host mount their war horses
and spur them hard the whole length of the pass;
and every man of them says to the other:
"If only we find Roland before he's killed,
we'll stand with him, and then we'll do some fighting!"   1805
What does it matter what they say? They are too late.

137.

It is the end of day, and full of light,
arms and armor are ablaze in the sun,
and fire flashes from hauberks and helmets,
and from those shields, painted fair with flowers,   1810
and from those lances, those gold-dressed gonfanons.
The Emperor rides on in rage and sorrow,
the men of France indignant and full of grief.
There is no man of them who does not weep,
they are in fear for the life of Roland.   1815
The King commands: seize Ganelon the Count!
and gave him over to the cooks of his house;
summons the master cook, their chief, Besgun:
"Guard him for me like the traitor he is:
he has betrayed the barons of my house."   1820
Besgun takes him, sets his kitchen comrades,
a hundred men, the best, the worst, on him;
and they tear out his beard and his mustache,
each one strikes him four good blows with his fist;
and they lay into him with cudgels and sticks,   1825
put an iron collar around his neck
and chain him up, as they would chain a bear;
dumped him, in dishonor, on a packhorse,
and guard him well till they give him back to Charles.

138.

High are the hills, and tenebrous, and vast, AOI.   1830
the valleys deep, the raging waters swift;
to the rear, to the front, the trumpets sound:
they answer the lone voice of the olifant.
The Emperor rides on, rides on in fury,
the men of France in grief and indignation.   1835
There is no man who does not weep and wail,
and they pray God: protect the life of Roland
till they come, one great host, into the field
and fight at Roland's side like true men all.
What does it matter what they pray? It does no good.   1840
They are too late, they cannot come in time. AOI.

139.

King Charles the Great rides on, a man in wrath,
his great white beard spread out upon his hauberk.
All the barons of France ride spurring hard,
there is no man who does not wail, furious   1845
not to be with Roland, the captain count,
who stands and fights the Saracens of Spain,
so set upon, I cannot think his soul abides.
God! those sixty men who stand with him, what men!
No king, no captain ever stood with better. AOI.   1850

is this the song?

140.

Roland looks up on the mountains and slopes,
sees the French dead, so many good men fallen,
and weeps for them, as a great warrior weeps:
"Barons, my lords, may God give you his grace,
may he grant Paradise to all your souls,   1855
make them lie down among the holy flowers.
I never saw better vassals than you.
All the years you've served me, and all the times,
the mighty lands you conquered for Charles our King!
The Emperor raised you for this terrible hour!   1860
Land of France, how sweet you are, native land,
laid waste this day, ravaged, made a desert.
Barons of France, I see you die for me,
and I, your lord—I cannot protect you.
May God come to your aid, that God who never failed.   1865
Oliver, brother, now I will not fail *you*.
I will die here—of grief, if no man kills me.
Lord, Companion, let us return and fight."

1843: The beard spread out upon the hauberk is a gesture of defiance toward the enemy. See below, lines 3122, 3318, 3520.

141.

Roland returned to his place on the field,
strikes—a brave man keeping faith—with Durendal,   1870
struck through Faldrun de Pui, cut him to pieces,
and twenty-four of the men they valued most;
no man will ever want his vengeance more!
As when the deer turns tail before the dogs,
so the pagans flee before Roland the Count.   1875
Said the Archbishop: "You! Roland! What a fighter!
Now that's what every knight must have in him
who carries arms and rides on a fine horse:
he must be strong, a savage, when he's in battle;
for otherwise, what's he worth? Not four cents!   1880
Let that four-cent man be a monk in some minster,
and he can pray all day long for our sins."
Roland replies: "Attack, do not spare them!"
And with that word the Franks began again.
There was a heavy loss of Christian men.   1885

142.

When a man knows there'll be no prisoners,
what will that man not do to defend himself!
And so the Franks fight with the fury of lions.
Now Marsilion, the image of a baron,
mounted on that war horse he calls Gaignun,   1890
digs in his spurs, comes on to strike Bevon,
who was the lord of Beaune and of Dijon;
smashes his shield, rips apart his hauberk,
knocks him down, dead, no need to wound him more.
And then he killed Yvorie and Yvon,   1895
and more: he killed Gerard of Rousillon.
Roland the Count is not far away now,
said to the pagan: "The Lord God's curse on you!
You kill my companions, how you wrong me!
You'll feel the pain of it before we part,   1900
you will learn my sword's name by heart today";
comes on to strike—the image of a baron.
He has cut off Marsilion's right fist;
now takes the head of Jurfaleu the blond—
the head of Jurfaleu! Marsilion's son.   1905
The pagans cry: "Help, Mahumet! Help us!
Vengeance, our gods, on Charles! the man who set
these criminals on us in our own land,
they will not quit the field, they'll stand and die!"
And one said to the other: "Let *us* run then."   1910
And with that word, some hundred thousand flee.
Now try to call them back: they won't return. AOI.

143.
What does it matter? If Marsilion has fled,
his uncle has remained: the Algalife,
who holds Carthage, Alfrere, and Garmalie,   1915
and Ethiopia: a land accursed;
holds it immense black race under his power,
the huge noses, the enormous ears on them;
and they number more than fifty thousand.
These are the men who come riding in fury,   1920
and now they shout that pagan battle cry.
And Roland said: "Here comes our martyrdom;
I see it now; we have not long to live.
But let the world call any man a traitor
        who does not make them pay before he dies!
My lords, attack! Use those bright shining swords!   1925
Fight a good fight for your deaths and your lives,
let no shame touch sweet France because of us!
When Charles my lord comes to this battlefield
and sees how well we punished these Saracens,
finds fifteen of their dead for one of ours,   1930
I'll tell you what he will do: he will bless us." AOI.

144.
When Roland sees that unbelieving race,
those hordes and hordes blacker than blackest ink—
no shred of white on them except their teeth—
then said the Count: "I see it clearly now,   1935
we die today: it is there before us.
Men of France, strike! I will start it once more."
Said Oliver: "God curse the slowest man."
And with that word, the French strike into battle.

145.
The Saracens, when they saw these few French,   1940
looked at each other, took courage, and presumed,
telling themselves: "The Emperor is wrong!"
The Algalife rides a great sorrel horse,
digs into it with his spurs of fine gold,
strikes Oliver, from behind, in the back,   1945
shattered the white hauberk upon his flesh,
drove his spear through the middle of his chest;
and speaks to him: "Now you feel you've been struck!
Your great Charles doomed you when he left you in this pass.
That man wronged us, he must not boast of it.   1950
I've avenged all our dead in you alone!"

1914. **The Algalife**: The Caliph, Marsilion's uncle, whom Ganelon lied about to
Charlemagne. See lines 680–91 (also lines 453, 493, 505).

146.
Oliver feels: he has been struck to death;
grips Halteclere, that steel blade shining, strikes
on the gold-dressed pointed helm of the Algalife,
sends jewels and flowers crackling down to the earth,   1955
into the head, into the little teeth;
draws up his flashing sword, casts him down, dead,
and then he says: "Pagan, a curse on you!
If only I could say Charles has lost nothing—
but no woman, no lady you ever knew   1960
will hear you boast, in the land you came from,
that you could take one thing worth a cent from me,
or do me harm, or do any man harm";
then cries out to Roland to come to his aid. AOI.

147.
Oliver feels he is wounded to death,   1965
will never have his fill of vengeance, strikes,
as a baron strikes, where they are thickest,
cuts through their lances, cuts through those buckled shields,
through feet, through fists, through saddles, and through flanks.
Had you seen him, cutting the pagans limb   1970
from limb, casting one corpse down on another,
you would remember a brave man keeping faith.
Never would he forget Charles' battle-cry,
Munjoie! he shouts, that mighty voice ringing;
calls to Roland, to his friend and his peer: 1975
"Lord, Companion, come stand beside me now.
We must part from each other in pain today." AOI.

148.
Roland looks hard into Oliver's face,
it is ashen, all its color is gone,
the bright red blood streams down upon his body,   1980
Oliver's blood spattering on the earth.
"God!" said the Count, "I don't know what to do,
Lord, Companion, your fight is finished now.
There'll never be a man the like of you.
Sweet land of France, today you will be stripped   1985
of good vassals, laid low, a fallen land!
The Emperor will suffer the great loss";
faints with that word, mounted upon his horse. AOI.

149.

Here is Roland, lords, fainted on his horse,
and Oliver the Count, wounded to death: 1990
he has lost so much blood, his eyes are darkened—
he cannot see, near or far, well enough
to recognize a friend or enemy:
struck when he came upon his companion,
strikes on his helm, adorned with gems in gold,   1995
cuts down straight through, from the point to the nasal,
but never harmed him, he never touched his head.
Under this blow, Count Roland looked at him;
and gently, softly now, he asks of him:
"Lord, Companion, do you mean to do this?   2000
It is Roland, who always loved you greatly.
You never declared that we were enemies."
Said Oliver: "Now I hear it is you—
I don't see you, may the Lord God see you.
Was it you that I struck? Forgive me then."   2005
Roland replies: "I am not harmed, not harmed,
I forgive you, Friend, here and before God."
And with that word, each bowed to the other.
And this is the love, lords, in which they parted.

150.

Oliver feels: death pressing hard on him;   2010
his two eyes turn, roll up into his head,
all hearing is lost now, all sight is gone;
gets down on foot, stretches out on the ground,
cries out now and again: *mea culpa!*
his two hands joined, raised aloft toward heaven,   2015
he prays to God: grant him His Paradise;
and blesses Charles, and the sweet land of France,
his companion, Roland, above all men.
The heart fails him, his helmet falls away,
the great body settles upon the earth.   2020
The Count is dead, he stands with us no longer.
Roland, brave man, weeps for him, mourns for him,
you will not hear a man of greater sorrow.

1996. **Nasal:** the nosepiece protruding down from the cone-shaped helmet.

151.

brotherly love? homosocial bond?

Roland the Count, when he sees his friend dead,
lying stretched out, his face against the earth,   2025
softly, gently, begins to speak the regret:
"Lord, Companion, you were brave and died for it.
We have stood side by side through days and years,
you never caused me harm, I never wronged you;
when you are dead, to be alive pains me."   2030
And with that word the lord of marches faints
upon his horse, which he calls Veillantif.
He is held firm by his spurs of fine gold,
whichever way he leans, he cannot fall.

152.

Before Roland could recover his senses   2035
and come out of his faint, and be aware,
a great disaster had come forth before him:
the French are dead, he has lost every man
except the Archbishop, and Gautier de l'Hum,
who has come back, down from that high mountain: 2040
he has fought well, he fought those men of Spain.
His men are dead, the pagans finished them;
flees now down to these valleys, he has no choice,
and calls on Count Roland to come to his aid:
"My noble Count, my brave lord, where are you?   2045
I never feared whenever you were there.
It is Walter: I conquered Maëlgut,
my uncle is Droün, old and gray: your Walter
and always dear to you for the way I fought;
and I have fought this time: my lance is shattered,   2050
my good shield pierced, my hauberk's meshes broken;
and I am wounded, a lance struck through my body.
I will die soon, but I sold myself dear."
And with that word, Count Roland has heard him,
he spurs his horse, rides spurring to his man. AOI.   2055

2026. **to speak the regret**: what follows is a formal and customary lament for the
dead.

153.

Roland in pain, maddened with grief and rage:
rushes where they are thickest and strikes again,
strikes twenty men of Spain, strikes twenty dead,
and Walter six, and the Archbishop five.
The pagans say: "Look at those criminals!   2060
Now take care, Lords, they don't get out alive,
only a traitor will not attack them now!
Only a coward will let them save their skins!"
And then they raise their hue and cry once more,
rush in on them, once more, from every side. AOI.   2065

154.

Count Roland was always a noble warrior,
Gautier de l'Hum is a fine mounted man,
the Archbishop, a good man tried and proved:
not one of them will ever leave the others;
strike, where they are thickest, at the pagans.   2070
A thousand Saracens get down on foot,
and forty thousand more are on their mounts:
and I tell you, not one will dare come close,
they throw, and from afar, lances and spears,
wigars and darts, mizraks, javelins, pikes.   2075
With the first blows they killed Gautier de l'Hum
and struck Turpin of Reims, pierced through his shield,
broke the helmet on him, wounded his head;
ripped his hauberk, shattered its rings of mail,
and pierced him with four spears in his body,   2080
the war horse killed under him; and now there comes
great pain and rage when the Archbishop falls. AOI.

155.

Turpin of Reims, when he feels he is unhorsed,
struck to the earth with four spears in his body,
quickly, brave man, leaps to his feet again;   2085
his eyes find Roland now, he runs to him
and says one word: "See! I'm not finished yet!
What good vassal ever gives up alive!";
and draws Almace, his sword, that shining steel!
and strikes, where they are thickest, a thousand blows, and   2090
       more.
Later, Charles said: Turpin had spared no one;
he found four hundred men prostrate around him,
some of them wounded, some pierced from front to back,
some with their heads hacked off. So says the Geste,
and so says one who was there, on that field,   2095
the baron Saint Gilles, for whom God performs miracles,
who made the charter setting forth these great things
        in the Church of Laon. Now any man
who does not know this much understands nothing.

156.

Roland the Count fights well and with great skill,
but he is hot, his body soaked with sweat;   2100
has a great wound in his head, and much pain,
his temple broken because he blew the horn.   *may come*
But he must know whether King Charles will come;   *too late*
draws out the olifant, sounds it, so feebly.
The Emperor drew to a halt, listened.   2105
"Seigneurs," he said, "it goes badly for us—
My nephew Roland falls from our ranks today.
I hear it in the horn's voice: he hasn't long.
Let every man who wants to be with Roland
ride fast! Sound trumpets! Every trumpet in this host!"   2110
Sixty thousand, on these words, sound, so high
the mountains sound, and the valleys resound.
The pagans hear: it is no joke to them;
cry to each other: "We're getting Charles on us!"

2095–98: Saint Gilles of Provence: These lines explain how the story of Rencesvals
could be told after all who had fought there died. See Ramón Menéndez Pidal, *La
Chanson de Roland et la tradition épique des Francs*, 2d ed. (Paris, 1960), p. 283;
Bédier, *La Chanson de Roland commentée*, p. 26.

157.

The pagans say: "The Emperor is coming, AOI.   2115
listen to their trumpets—it is the French!
If Charles comes back, it's all over for us,
if Roland lives, this war begins again
and we have lost our land, we have lost Spain."
Some four hundred, helmets laced on, assemble,   2120
some of the best, as they think, on that field.
They storm Roland, in one fierce, bitter attack.
And now Count Roland has some work on his hands. AOI.

158.

Roland the Count, when he sees them coming,
how strong and fierce and alert he becomes!   2125
He will not yield to them, not while he lives.
He rides the horse they call Veillantif, spurs,
digs into it with his spurs of fine gold,
and rushes at them all where they are thickest,
the Archbishop—that Turpin!—at his side.   2130
Said one man to the other: "Go at it, friend.
The horns we heard were the horns of the French,
King Charles is coming back with all his strength."

159.

Roland the Count never loved a coward,
a blusterer, an evil-natured man,   2135
a man on horse who was not a good vassal.
And now he called to Archbishop Turpin:
"You are on foot, Lord, and here I am mounted,
and so, here I take my stand: for love of you.
We'll take whatever comes, the good and bad,   *homosocial*   2140
together, Lord: no one can make me leave you.   *bond*
They will learn our swords' names today in battle,
the name of Almace, the name of Durendal!"
Said the Archbishop: "Let us strike or be shamed!
Charles is returning, and he brings our revenge."   2145

2131–33. These lines could be spoken either by Roland and the Archbishop or by the pagans.

160.

Say the pagans: "We were all born unlucky!
The evil day that dawned for us today!
We have lost our lords and peers, and now comes Charles—
that Charlemagne!—with his great host. Those trumpets!
that shrill sound on us—the trumpets of the French!   2150
And the loud roar of that Munjoie! This Roland
is a wild man, he is too great a fighter—
What man of flesh and blood can ever hope
to bring him down? Let us cast at him, and leave him there."
And so they did: arrows, wigars, darts,   2155
lances and spears, javelots dressed with feathers;
struck Roland's shield, pierced it, broke it to pieces,
ripped his hauberk, shattered its rings of mail,
but never touched his body, never his flesh.
They wounded Veillantif in thirty places,   2160
struck him dead, from afar, under the Count.
The pagans flee, they leave the field to him.
Roland the Count stood alone, on his feet. AOI.

161.

The pagans flee, in biterness and rage,
strain every nerve running headlong toward Spain,.   2165
and Count Roland has no way to chase them,
he has lost Veillantif, his battle horse;
he has no choice, left alone there on foot.
He went to the aid of Archbishop Turpin,
unlaced the gold-dressed helmet, raised it from his head,   2170
lifted away his bright, light coat of mail,
cut his under tunic into some lengths,
stilled his great wounds with thrusting on the strips;
then held him in his arms, against his chest,
and laid him down, gently, on the green grass;   2175
and softly now Roland entreated him:
"My noble lord, I beg you, give me leave:
our companions, whom we have loved so dearly,
are all dead now, we must not abandon them.
I want to look for them, know them once more,   2180
and set them in ranks, side by side, before you."
Said the Archbishop: "Go then, go and come back.
The field is ours, thanks be to God, yours and mine."

Laisses 161ff. This respite granted to Roland and Turpin after the pagans have fled and
before these heroes die is an act of overwhelming grace, one of the poem's many
lyrical arrests, and the sign of the two men's blessedness.

162.

So Roland leaves him, walks the field all alone,
seeks in the valleys, and seeks in the mountains.   2185
He found Gerin, and Gerer his companion,
and then he found Berenger and Otun,
Anseïs and Sansun, and on that field
he found Gerard the old of Roussillon;
and caried them, brave man, all, one by one,   2190
came back to the Archbishop with these French dead,
and set them down in ranks before his knees.
The Archbishop cannot keep from weeping,
raises his hand and makes his benediction;
and said: "Lords, Lords, it was your terrible hour.   2195
May the Glorious God set all your souls
among the holy flowers of Paradise!
Here is my own death, Lords, pressing on me,
I shall not see our mighty Emperor."

163.

And Roland leaves, seeks in the field again;   2200
he has found Oliver, his companion,
held him tight in his arms against his chest;
came back to the Archbishop, laid Oliver
down on a shield among the other dead.
The Archbishop absolved him, signed him with the Cross.   2205
And pity now and rage and grief increase;
and Roland says: "Oliver, dear companion,
you were the son of the great duke Renier,
who held the march of the vale of Runers.
Lord, for shattering lances, for breaking shields,   2210
for making men great with presumption weak with fright,
for giving life and counsel to good men,
for striking fear in that unbelieving race,
no warrior on earth surpasses you."

164.

Roland the Count, when he sees his peers dead,   2215
and Oliver, whom he had good cause to love,
felt such grief and pity, he begins to weep;
and his face lost its color with what he felt:
a pain so great he cannot keep on standing,
he has no choice, falls fainting to the ground.   2220
Said the Archbishop: "Baron, what grief for you."

165.

The Archbishop, when he saw Roland faint,
felt such pain then as he had never felt;
stretched out his hand and grasped the olifant.
At Rencesvals there is a running stream: 2225
he will go there and fetch some water for Roland;
and turns that way, with small steps, staggering;
he is too weak, he cannot go ahead,
he has no strength: all the blood he has lost.
In less time than a man takes to cross a little field   2230
that great heart fails, he falls forward, falls down;
and Turpin's death comes crushing down on him.

166.

Roland the Count recovers from his faint,
gets to his feet, but stands with pain and grief;
looks down the valley, looks up the mountain, sees: 2235
on the green grass, beyond his companions,
that great and noble man down on the ground,
the Archbishop, whom God sent in His name;
who confesses his sins, lifts up his eyes,
holds up his hands joined together to heaven,   2240
and prays to God: grant him that Paradise.
Turpin is dead, King Charles' good warrior.
In great battles, in beautiful sermons
he was ever a champion against the pagans.
Now God grant Turpin's soul His holy blessing. AOI.   2245

167.

Roland the Count sees the Archbishop down,
sees the bowels fallen out of his body,
and the brain boiling down from his forehead.
Turpin has crossed his hands upon his chest
beneath the collarbone, those fine white hands.   2250
Roland speaks the lament, after the custom
followed in his land: aloud, with all his heart:
"My noble lord, you great and well-born warrior,
I commend you today to the God of Glory,
whom none will ever serve with a sweeter will.
Since the Apostles no prophet the like of you   2255
arose to keep the faith and draw men to it.
May your soul know no suffering or want,
and behold the gate open to Paradise."

2255. Compare Deuteronomy, 34:10.

168.
Now Roland feels that death is very near.
His brain comes spilling out through his two ears;   2260
prays to God for his peers: let them be called;
and for himself, to the angel Gabriel;
took the oliphant: there must be no reproach!
took Durendal his sword in his other hand,
and farther than a crossbow's farthest shot   2265
he walks toward Spain, into a fallow land,
and climbs a hill: there beneath two fine trees
stand four great blocks of stone, all are of marble;
and he fell back, to earth, on the green grass,
has fainted there, for death is very near.   2270

169.
High are the hills, and high, high are the trees;
there stand four blocks of stone, gleaming of marble.
Count Roland falls fainting on the green grass,
and is watched, all this time, by a Saracen:
who has feigned death and lies now with the others,   2275
has smeared blood on his face and on his body;
and quickly now gets to his feet and runs—
a handsome man, strong, brave, and so crazed with pride
that he does something mad and dies for it:
laid hands on Roland, and on the arms of Roland,   2280
and cried: "Conquered! Charles's nephew conquered!
I'll carry this sword home to Arabia!"
As he draws it, the Count begins to come round.

170.
Now Roland feels: *someone taking his sword!*
opened his eyes, and had one word for him: 2285
"I don't know you, you aren't one of ours";
grasps that olifant that he will never lose,
strikes on the helm beset with gems in gold,
shatters the steel, and the head, and the bones,
sent his two eyes flying out of his head,   2290
dumped him over stretched out at his feet dead;
and said: "You nobody! how could you dare
lay hands on me—rightly or wrongly: how?
Who'll hear of this and not call you a fool?
Ah! the bell-mouth of the olifant is smashed,   2295
the crystal and the gold fallen away."

171.

Now Roland the Count feels: his sight is gone;
gets on his feet, draws on his final strength,
the color on his face lost now for good.
Before him stands a rock; and on that dark rock   2300
in rage and bitterness he strikes ten blows:
the steel blade grates, it will not break, it stands unmarked.
"Ah!" said the Count, "Blessed Mary, your help!
Ah Durendal, good sword, your unlucky day,
for I am lost and cannot keep you in my care.   2305
The battles I have won, fighting with you,
the mighty lands that holding you I conquered,
that Charles rules now, our King, whose beard is white!
Now you fall to another: it must not be
        a man who'd run before another man!
For a long while a good vassal held you: 2310
there'll never be the like in France's holy land."

172.

Roland strikes down on that rock of Cerritania:
the steel blade grates, will not break, stands unmarked.
Now when he sees he can never break that sword,
Roland speaks the lament, in his own presence: 2315
"Ah Durendal, how beautiful and bright!
so full of light, all on fire in the sun!
King Charles was in the vales of Moriane
when God sent his angel and commanded him,
from heaven, to give you to a captain count.   2320
That great and noble King girded it on me.
And with this sword I won Anjou and Brittany,
I won Poitou, I won Le Maine for Charles,
and Normandy, that land where men are free,
I won Provence and Aquitaine with this,   2325
and Lombardy, and every field of Romagna,
I won Bavaria, and all of Flanders,
all of Poland, and Bulgaria, for Charles,
Constantinople, which pledged him loyalty,
and Saxony, where he does as he wills;   2330
and with this sword I won Scotland and Ireland,
and England, his chamber, his own domain—
the lands, the nations I conquered with this sword,
for Charles, who rules them now, whose beard is white!
Now, for this sword, I am pained with grief and rage: 2335
Let it not fall to pagans! Let me die first!
Our Father God, save France from that dishonor."

173.

Roland the Count strikes down on a dark rock,
and the rock breaks, breaks more than I can tell,
and the blade grates, but Durendal will not break,   2340
the sword leaped up, rebounded toward the sky.
The Count, when he sees that sword will not be broken,
softly, in his own presence, speaks the lament:
"Ah Durendal, beautiful, and most sacred,
the holy relics in this golden pommel!   2345
Saint Peter's tooth and blood of Saint Basile,
a lock of hair of my lord Saint Denis, - St. of France
and a fragment of blessed Mary's robe:
your power must not fall to the pagans,
you must be served by Christian warriors.   2350
May no coward ever come to hold you!
It was with you I conquered those great lands
that Charles has in his keeping, whose beard is white,
the Emperor's lands, that make him rich and strong."

174.

Now Roland feels: death coming over him,   2355
death descending from his temples to his heart.
He came running underneath a pine tree
and there stretched out, face down, on the green grass,
lays beneath him his sword and the olifant.
He turned his head toward the Saracen hosts,   2360
and this is why: with all his heart he wants
King Charles the Great and all his men to say,
he died, that noble Count, a conqueror;
makes confession, beats his breast often, so feebly,
offers his glove, for all his sins, to God. AOI.   2365

175.

Now Roland feels that his time has run out;
he lies on a steep hill, his face toward Spain;
and with one of his hands he beat his breast:
"Almighty God, *mea culpa* in thy sight,
forgive my sins, both the great and the small,   2370
sins I committed from the hour I was born
until this day, in which I lie struck down."
And then he held his right glove out to God.
Angels descend from heaven and stand by him. AOI.

2369. See Psalm 51:4.

176.

Count Roland lay stretched out beneath a pine;   2375
he turned his face toward the land of Spain,
began to remember many many things now:
how many lands, brave man, he had conquered;
and he remembered: sweet France, the men of his line,
remembered Charles, his lord, who fostered him: 2380
cannot keep, remembering, from weeping, sighing;
but would not be unmindful of himself:
he confesses his sins, prays God for mercy:
"Loyal Father, you who never failed us,
who resurrected Saint Lazarus from the dead,   2385
and saved your servant Daniel from the lions:
now save the soul of me from every peril
for the sins I committed while I still lived."
Then he held out his right glove to his Lord:
Saint Gabriel took the glove from his hand.   2390
He held his head bowed down upon his arm,
he is gone, his two hands joined, to his end.
Then God sent him his angel Cherubin
and Saint Michael, angel of the sea's Peril;
and with these two there came Saint Gabriel: 2395
they bear Count Roland's soul to Paradise.

177.

Roland is dead, God has his soul in heaven.
The Emperor rides into Rencesvals;
there is no passage there, there is no track,
no empty ground, not an elle, not one foot,   2400
that does not bear French dead or pagan dead.
King Charles cries out: "Dear Nephew, where are you?
Where is the Archbishop? Count Oliver?
Where is Gerin, his companion Gerer?
Where is Otun, where is Count Berenger,   2405
Yves and Yvoire, men I have loved so dearly?
What has become of Engeler the Gascon,
Sansun the Duke, and Anseïs, that fighter?
Where is Gerard the Old of Roussillon,
and the Twelve Peers, whom I left in these passes?"   2410
And so forth—what's the difference? No one answered.
"God!" said the King, "how much I must regret
I was not here when the battle began";
pulls his great beard, a man in grief and rage.
His brave knights weep, their eyes are filled with tears,   2415
twenty thousand fall fainting to the ground;
Duke Naimon feels the great pity of it.

178.

There is no knight or baron on that field
who does not weep in bitterness and grief;
for they all weep: for their sons, brothers, nephew,   2420
weep for their friends, for their sworn men and lords;
the mass of them fall fainting to the ground.
Here Naimon proved a brave and useful man:
he was the first to urge the Emperor:
"Look ahead there, two leagues in front of us,   2425
you can see the dust rising on those wide roads:
the pagan host—and how many they are!
After them now! Ride! Avenge this outrage!"
"Oh! God!" said Charles, "look how far they have gotten!
Lord, let me have my right, let me have honor,   2430
they tore from me the flower of sweet France."
The King commands Gebuïn and Othon,
Thibaut of Reims and Count Milun his cousin:
"Now guard this field, the valleys, the mountains,
let the dead lie, all of them, as they are,   2435
let no lion, let no beast come near them,
let no servant, let no groom come near them,
I command you, let no man come near these dead
until God wills we come back to this field."
And they reply, gently, and in great love: 2440
"Just Emperor, dear Lord, we shall do that."
They keep with them a thousand of their knights. AOI.

179.

The Emperor has his high-pitched trumpets sound,
and then he rides, brave man, with his great host.
They made the men of Spain show them their heels,   2445
and they keep after them, all as one man.
When the King sees the twilight faltering,
he gets down in a meadow on the green grass,
lies on the ground, prays to the Lord his God
to make the sun stand still for him in heaven,   2450
hold back the night, let the day linger on.
Now comes the angel always sent to speak with Charles;
and the angel at once commanded him:
"Charles, ride: God knows. The light will not fail you.
God knows that you have lost the flower of France.   2455
You can take vengeance now on that criminal race."
The Emperor, on that word, mounts his horse. AOI.

2452. **The angel always sent to speak with Charles:** Gabriel. Compare *laisses* 185, 203, 291, and others. On the story of Joshua as the model for this episode, see Menéndez Pidal, *La Chanson de Roland et la tradition épique*, p. 318.

180.

God made great miracles for Charlemagne,
for on that day in heaven the sun stood still.
The pagans flee, the Franks keep at their heels,   2460
catch up with them in the Vale Tenebrous,
chase them on spurring hard to Saragossa,
and always killing them, striking with fury;
cut off their paths, the widest roads away:
the waters of the Ebro lie before them,   2465
very deep, an amazing sight, and swift;
and there is no boat, no barge, no dromond, no galley.
They call on Tervagant, one of their gods.
Then they jump in, but no god is with them:
those in full armor, the ones who weigh the most,   2470
sank down, and they were many, to the bottom;
the others float downstream: the luckiest ones,
who fare best in those waters, have drunk so much,
they all drown there, struggling, it is amazing.
The French cry out: "Curse the day you saw Roland!" AOI.   2475

181.

When Charlemagne sees all the pagans dead,
many struck down, the great mass of them drowned—
the immense spoils his knights win from that battle!—
the mighty King at once gets down on foot,
lies on the ground, and gives thanks to the Lord.   2480
When he stands up again, the sun has set.
Said the Emperor: "It is time to make camp.
It is late now to return to Rencesvals;
our horses are worn out, they have no strength—
take off their saddles, the bridles on their heads,   2485
let them cool down and rest in these meadows."
The Franks reply: "Yes, as you well say, Lord." AOI.

182.

The Emperor commands them to make camp.
The French dismount into that wilderness;
they have removed the saddles from their horses,   2490
and the bridles, dressed in gold, from their heads,
free them to the meadows and the good grass;
and that is all the care they can give them.
Those who are weary sleep on the naked earth;
and all sleep, they set no watch that night.   2495

183.
The Emperor lay down in a meadow,
puts his great spear, brave man, beside his head;
he does not wish, on this night, to disarm:
he has put on his bright, brass-sewn hauberk,
laced on his helm, adorned with gems in gold,   2500
and girded on Joiuse, there never was its like:
each day it shines with thirty different lights.
There are great things that we can say about the lance
with which Our Lord was wounded on the Cross:
thanks be to God, Charles has its iron point,   2505
he had it mounted in that sword's golden pommel.
For this honor, and for this mighty grace,
the name Joiuse was given to that sword.
Brave men of France must never forget this:
from this sword's name they get their cry Munjoie!   2510
This is why no nation can withstand them.

184.
The night is clear, the moon is shining bright,
Charles lies down in grief and pain for Roland,
and for Oliver, it weighs down on him hard,
for the Twelve Peers, for all the men of France   2515
whom he left dead, covered with blood, at Rencesvals;
and cannot keep from weeping, wailing aloud,
and prays to God: lead their souls to safety.
His weariness is great, for his pain is great;
he has fallen asleep, he cannot go on.   2520
Through all the meadows now the Franks are sleeping.
There is no horse that has the strength to stand:
if one wants grass, he grazes lying down.
He has learned much who knows much suffering.

185.
Charlemagne sleeps, a man worn out with pain.   2525
God sent Saint Gabriel to him that night
with this command: watch over the Emperor.
All through the night the angel stands at his head;
and in a vision he brought the King dread tidings
of a great battle soon to come against him: 2530
revealed to him its grave signification:
Charles raised his eyes and looked up to the sky,
he sees the thunder, the winds, the blasts of ice,
the hurricanes, the dreadful tempests,
the fires and flames made ready in the sky.   2535
And suddenly all things fall on his men.
Their lances burn, the wood of ash and apple,
and their shields burn down to their golden bosses,
the shafts of their sharp spears burst into pieces,
then the grating of hauberks, helmets of steel.   2540
He sees his warriors in great distress—
leopards and bears furious to devour them,
serpents, vipers, dragons, demons of hell,
swarms of griffins, thirty thousand and more,
and all come swooping down upon the French;   2545
and the French cry: "Charlemagne, come help us!"
The King is filled with rage and pain and pity,
wants to go there, but something blocks his way:
out of a wood a great lion coming at him,
it is tremendous, wild, and great with pride: 2550
seeks the King's very body, attacks the King!
and they lock arms, King and lion, to fight,
and still he cannot tell who strikes, who falls.
The Emperor sleeps, his dream does not wake him.

186.
And after this he was shown another vision: 2555
he was in France, at Aix, on a stone step,
and two chains in his hands holding a bear;
from the Ardennes he saw thirty bears coming,
and each of them was speaking like a man;
they said to him: "Lord, give him back to us,   2560
you must not keep him longer, it is not right;
he is our kin, we must deliver him."
From his palace a greyhound now, running,
leaps on the greatest bear among them all,
on the green grass beyond his companions,   2565
there the King sees an amazing struggle
but cannot tell who conquers, who goes down.
These are the things God's angel showed this baron.
Charles sleeps until the morning and the bright day.

187.

King Marsilion flees to Saragossa,   2570
dismounts in shadow beneath an olive tree,
gives up his sword, his helmet, his hauberk,
lies down in shame, on the green grass, outraged:
he has lost his right hand, cleanly cut off,
faints from the loss of blood and chokes with pain.   2575
And before him stands his wife Bramimunde,
who weeps and wails, the fury of her lament!
and thirty thousand men, and more, with her,
cursing King Charles and the sweet land of France.
They rush into a crypt to Apolin   2580
and rail at him, disfigure him to vileness:
"Eh! you bad god, the shame you have done us!
Why did you let our king be beaten to dishhonor?
You give bad wages to men who serve you well."
They tear away his scepter and his crown,   2585
lay hands on him atop a lofty column
and throw him to the ground beneath their feet,
and beat him with big sticks, smash him to pieces;
and tear from Tervagant his great carbuncle,
and throw the god Mahum into a ditch,   2590
and pigs and dogs bite him and befoul him.

188.

King Marsilion has recovered from his faint,
has himself borne into his vaulted chamber,
a room inscribed and adorned in every color.
And Bramimunde the Queen weeps over him,   2595
tears at her hair, calls herself miserable,
and now she cries at the top of her voice:
"Ah, Saragossa, today you have been stripped
of the great King who had you in his keeping.
Those gods of ours! Every one was a traitor,   2600
deserting him in the battle this morning!
The Amiral will·prove he is a coward
unless he fights that host of iron men—
such savage men, they've no thought for their lives.
That Emperor! that flowering white beard!   2605
he is a brave man, and wild! a reckless man!
If there's a battle, that man will never run.
And no one kills him! The shame of it, the outrage!"

2602. **The Amiral**: Baligant, Marsilion's lord, and the supreme lord of all heathen-dom.

189.
The Emperor with all his mighty host
has warred seven full years in the land of Spain,   2610
takes many castles, takes city upon city.
King Marsilion does everything to stop him:
in that first year he had his letters sealed
and sent to Baligant in Babylonia—
that is the Amiral, that is the old man,   2615
the ancient who outlived Homer and Virgil!—:
Let that great lord deliver Saragossa,
for otherwise the King will quit his gods,
abandon the idols he has adored,
and take *their* law, the holy Christian faith,   2620
and willingly make peace with Charlemagne.
Baligant is far away, he has delayed.
From forty realms he calls his people forth;
he has prepared his great fast-sailing dromonds,
warships, barges, galleys, ships without number.   2625
There is a seaport below Alexandria:
he had all his vast fleet made ready there.
This is in May, on the first day of summer:
he thrust his mighty hosts upon the sea.

190.
Great are the hosts of that enemy race.   2630
They steer ever onward, by sail, by oar.
Atop the masts and on the ships' high prows
carbuncles shine, lanterns on lanterns shine,
and cast forth from on high such blazing light
the sea is fairer for it, in the dark night;   2635
and as they come upon the land of Spain,
all that country glows with that pagan light.
The news of their coming reaches Marsilion. AOI.

191.
The pagan hosts will not rest on their way,
they leave the sea and sail into fresh water,   2640
they pass Marbrise, they pass Marbrose, sail on,
steer all their ships upstream upon the Ebro;
carbuncles shine, lanterns on lanterns shine,
all the night through they give the pagans light.
On that same day they come to Saragossa. AOI.   2645

192.

The day is clear, the sun is shining bright.
The Amiral descended from his ship,
Espaneliz walks humbly on his right,
and in his train follow seventeen kings
and dukes and counts, I cannot tell their number.   2650
Amid a field, beneath a laurel tree,
on the green grass, they spread white silk brocade,
set down on this the ruler's ivory chair;
and there he sits, the pagan Baligant.
All the others have remained on their feet.   2655
And the lord of them all was first to speak;
"Listen to me, you brave and noble knights:
Charlemagne the King, Emperor of the Franks,
has no right to eat unless I tell him to.
He has made war on me all over Spain;   2660
now I will seek him out in his sweet France.
There'll be no rest for me till he is dead
or lying at my feet begging to live";
strikes his right glove, for a sign, on his knee.

193.

After these words Baligant firmly swore   2665
he would not fail, for all the gold under heaven,
to go to Aix, the seat of Charlemagne's justice.
His men praise him, give him just this advice.
Then he called forth two of his warriors,
one Clarifan, the other Clariën: 2670
"You are both sons of King Maltraïen,
who always went as my willing messenger.
I command you, go to Saragossa,
and in my name inform Marsilion
I have come to his aid against the French: 2675
there'll be a battle, once I've decided where.
Give him this gold-dressed glove, folded as sign:
let the King put this glove on his right hand.
Then give him this gold scepter, and let him come
here before me to acknowledge his fief.   2680
I'm bound for France to bring the war to Charles:
if he does not throw himself on my mercy,
lie at my feet renouncing the Christian faith,
I'll take his crown, I'll tear it from his head."
The pagans answer: "That is well spoken, Lord."   2685

194.

Said Baligant: "Lords, time for you to ride!
One bear the glove, the other man the staff."
And they reply: "Dear Lord, we shall do that."
They rode and rode till they reach Saragossa,
pass through ten gates and ride across four bridges   2690
and through the streets where the townspeople live.
As they approach, on the heights of the city,
round the palace they heard a great murmur:
swarms of that pagan race are gathered there,
they weep and shout, take their grief into the street,   2695
lament their gods, Tervagant and Mahum
and Apollin, whom they no longer have,
cry to each other: "What will become of us?
Destruction and dishonor! You and I are finished!
Marsilion our King is lost to us—   2700
yesterday Count Roland cut off his hand;
and Jurfaleu the blond—gone from us forever.
They'll have all Spain under their flag today!"
The messengers dismount at the stone block.

195.

They leave their horses under an olive tree;   2705
there were two Saracens who took the reins.
The messengers held each other by their cloaks,
then they climbed up to that towering palace.
And as they entered the king's high-vaulted chamber,
in perfect love they gave the worst of greetings: 2710
"May that Mahum who has us in his hands,
and Tervagant, and Apollin our lord
save this great King and watch over his Queen!"
Said Bramimunde: "What madness do I hear!
These gods of ours are failures, deserters!   2715
The miserable wonders those gods performed
at Rencesvals: they let our men be killed,
they abandoned my lord lying here in battle:
he lost his hand—he has no right hand now,
Count Roland cut it off, the strength of that man!   2720
Charles will have all of Spain in his two hands.
What will become of me, a wretched captive!
How I regret there is no man to kill me!" AOI.

196.

Said Clarïen: "Lady, don't go on so.
We bring you word from Baligant lord of pagans.   2725
He will, he says, protect Marsilion,
sends him these things as sign: his staff, his glove.
On the Ebro we have four thousand boats,
warships, barges, galleys that run the sea,
the great ships there—I could not count their number.   2730
The Amiral is strong, his force is great,
he'll go to France to seek out Charlemagne;
he has one plan: kill him or make him beg."
Said Bramimunde: "He need not go so far.
You'll find the Franks much closer—they are right here,   2735
he has been in this land for seven years!
He is a fighter, a brave man, the Emperor,
he will not quit the field, he will die first,
he ranks no king on earth above a child,
he is Charlemagne! he fears no living man."   2740

197.

"Now let that be," said King Marsilion;
and to the messengers: "Lords, speak to me.
Now you can see I lie here in death's grip,
and have no son, no daughter—I have no heir;
I did have one, last evening he was killed.   2745
Now tell my lord he must come to see me:
the right to Spain belongs to the Emir!
I renounce it, if he wants to claim it,
but then let him defend it against the French.
I'll tell him what to do with Charlemagne,   2750
he'll capture him by one month from today.
Bring the Emir the keys to Saragossa;
tell him: if he trusts me, he will not leave."
And they reply: "That is true, Lord, well spoken." AOI.

198.

Said Marsilion: "Charlemagne the Emperor   2755
has killed my men and laid waste to my land,
broken my cities, outraged them with his force;
last night he lay on the shores of the Ebro,
not seven leagues from here: I counted them.
Tell the Emir to lead his army there,   2760
say, in my name: let the battle be fought there."
He has given them the keys to Saragossa.
Both of the messengers bowed to the King;
they take their leave and on those words depart.

199.

The messengers are mounted on their horses   2765
and ride with all their speed out of the city,
come to the Amiral in great distress;
and they give him the keys to Saragossa.
Said Baligant: "Tell me what you have found.
Where is Marsilion? I sent for him."   2770
Said Clarïen: "He is wounded and dying.
It happened yesterday. The Emperor
was marching through the passes, bound for sweet France;
in the rear-guard was his honor and pride:
Count Roland, his nephew, was in that guard,   2775
and Oliver, and all of the Twelve Peers,
and twenty thousand French, every man armed.
King Marsilion attacked this rear-guard, brave man!
came face to face on that field with Roland:
the Count struck him with Durendal and cut   2780
the right hand clean away from his body;
and killed his son, whom he had loved so dearly,
and all the barons he had led into battle.
He had to flee, he could hold out no longer;
the Emperor pursued him all the way.   2785
The King sends you this word: come to his aid,
he gives you all rights to the Kingdom of Spain."
And Baligant begins to picture it,
and feels such pain that he nearly goes mad. AOI.

200.

"Lord Amiral," said Clarïen,   2790
"there was a battle yesterday at Rencesvals.
Roland is dead, and Oliver the Count,
and the Twelve Peers, who were so dear to Charles,
and twenty thousand French—that many dead.
And King Marsilion lost his right fist;   2795
the Emperor pursued him all the way:
in all that land there's not one fighting man
not put to death or drowned in the Ebro.
The French are camped on the shore of that river,
in this very country, so close to us   2800
that if you wish, there's no retreat for them."
The look of this on Baligant is wild,
he is joyful, he glories in his heart;
leaps to his feet from his ivory chair of state,
and now he cries: "My Barons, no more waiting!   2805
Come from the ships, mount up, and ride your horses!
If Charlemagne, that old man, does not run,
King Marsilion will be avenged today,
I'll bring him Charles's head for his right fist!"

201.

Pagans of Araby came from the ships,   2810
and they got on their mounts—horses and mules—
and then they rode, was it not theirs to ride?
The Amiral, who sent them on this march,
called Gemalfin, one of his dearest men:
"I command you, take charge of all my armies";   2815
and mounted his war horse, one of his bays,
and takes four dukes to ride the way with him,
and rode so long—behold Saragossa;
dismounted there by the great block of marble;
there were four counts who came to hold his stirrup.   2820
He climbs the steps to Marsilion's palace,
And Bramimunde comes running to meet him,
and said to him: "Why was I born for grief!
I have lost my lord, Sire, and in such shame!";
falls at his feet, the Emir raised her up,   2825
and both went up to the chamber in grief. AOI.

202.

King Marsilion, when he sees Baligant,
calls before him two Saracens of Spain:
"Now lift me in your arms and sit me up";
and took, with his left hand, one of his gloves.   2830
Said Marsilion: "Lord King and Amiral,
I now return all the lands of this realm,
and Saragossa, and its dependent fief,
For I am lost, and have lost all my people."
And he replies: "This pains me all the more.   2835
I may not stay here long to talk with you.
I am quite sure Charles will not wait for me;
nevertheless, I take this glove from you";
and feels great pain; and went away in tears; AOI.
comes down the steps from Marsilion's palace,   2840
leaps on his horse, rides spurring to his people;
and rode so hard, behold him in the front,
leading his people, shouting and shouting again:
"Come, Pagan Men, the Franks are escaping us!" AOI.

203.

On that morning, at the first light of dawn,   2845
Charlemagne the Emperor woke from his sleep.
Saint Gabriel, who guards him in the Lord's name,
raises his hand and signs him with the Cross.
The King arises, and he lays down his arms,
and so, throughout the host, all men disarm.   2850
Then they mount up and ride with all their strength
on these long ways and on these great wide roads.
And they shall see the fearful numbers of the dead
at Rencesvals, where the great battle was. AOI.

204.

King Charles has reached the field of Rencesvals;   2855
and comes upon the dead, and weeps for them;
said to the French: "Seigneurs, keep at a walk,
for I must ride ahead by myself now:
it is for my nephew, I would find him.
I was at Aix one day, at a high feast,   2860
there were my valiant knights, all of them boasting
of great assaults, the battles they would fight.
There was one thing that I heard Roland say:
he said he would not die in a strange land
before he'd passed beyond his men and peers,   2865
he'd turn his face toward the enemies' land
and so, brave man, would die a conqueror."
Farther ahead than one could hurl a stick,
beyond them all, he has gone up a hill.

205.

The Emperor, as he looks for his nephew,   2870
found in the meadow grass many fair flowers
so bright and red with the blood of our barons;
and he is moved, he cannot keep from weeping.
He came beneath two trees and knew it was
Roland who struck those blows on the three rocks;   2875
and sees his nephew stretched out on the green grass.
Who would wonder at his rage and sorrow?—
gets down on foot; he has come running hard,
and takes in his two hands Roland the Count,
and falls fainting, choked with grief, on his body.   2880

Laisse 203. This *laisse* continues the action of lines 2496–2502. It is the morning after
the battle of Rencesvals, and Charles awakens at the same time that Baligant comes to
Marsilion's palace (in *laisse* 201). See Segre, pp. 512, 561.

206.

The Emperor recovered from his faint.
Naimon the Duke, and Acelin the Count,
Gefrei d'Anjou, and Tierri his brother
help the King up, help him stand beneath a pine.
The King looks on the ground, sees his nephew;   2885
and he begins, most gently, the regret:
"Roland, dear friend, God have mercy on you.
No man has seen a warrior like you
for fighting on till the great battle ends.
This is the fall and the death of my honor."   2890
Charlemagne faints, cannot hold out against it. AOI.

207.

King Charles the Great recovered from his faint,
his four barons raise him up with their hands;
looks on the ground, sees where his nephew lies,
Roland's body, vivid with life, its color gone,   2895
his eyes rolled up, overflowing with shadows;
speaks the lament, in love and loyalty:
"Roland, dear friend, God set your soul in the flowers
of Paradise, among his Glorious!
Lord, the black hour of your coming to Spain!   2900
No day will pass that I feel no pain for you.
My strength will fail, and my joy in my strength,
I'll have no man to uphold my honor;
under heaven I cannot find one friend;
there's all my kin, but where is the like of you!"—   2905
pulls at his hair, pulls with his two hands full.
A hundred thousand Franks feel the grief of this,
the tears they weep are bitter, and they all weep. AOI.

208.

"Roland, dear friend, I shall go back to France:
when I am in Laon, my own domain,   2910
alien vassals will come from many realms,
and they will ask: 'Where is the captain Count?'
I shall tell them: dead in the land of Spain!
And I shall rule my land henceforth in grief,
no day will pass that I do not weep and mourn."   2915

2910. **Laon**: the capital of the last Carolingians.

209.

"Dear friend, brave man, Roland, your fair young life!
And when I am in Aix, in my chapel,
vassals will come, and they will ask for news.
I shall tell them: Amazing, terrible news!
My nephew's dead, who led me to my conquests.   2920
Then the Saxons will rise up against me,
Hungarians, Bulgars, infidel races,
men of Romagna, Apulia, Palermo,
nations of Africa and Califerne;
then begins the season of my pains and losses.   2925
Who will rise with your strength to lead my hosts
when you are dead, who always captained us?
Sweet land of France, made a wasteland today!
The pain, the rage I feel! Let me not live!";
and falls to tearing out his great white beard,   2930
and tears with both his hands the hair on his head.
A hundred thousand Franks fall to the earth.

210.

"Dear friend, Roland, the end of your good life!
Now may your soul be set in Paradise!
What man killed you? Killing you he shamed sweet France.   2935
I live on, wanting to die, I feel such pain
for the men of my house, who died for me.
May God grant me, may blessed Mary's Son,
before I reach the great defiles of Cize,
grant that my soul part today from my body   2940
and take its place beside my warriors' souls,
and my flesh be buried beside their flesh";
and weeps, tears fill his eyes, pulls his white beard.
Duke Naimon said: "The great grief of Charlemagne." AOI.

211.

"Lord Emperor," said Geoffrey of Anjou,   2945
"do not linger in this pain and grief, come,
let our men be sought out across the field,
whom the pagans of Spain killed in this battle;
let them be borne into a common grave."
And the King said: "So be it. Sound your horn." AOI.   2950

2935. No man killed Roland. He died because his temples burst from the effort of blowing the horn. France is not ruined or dishonored.

212.

Gefrei d'Anjou sounded his high-pitched horn.
The French dismount, Charles has commanded it.
And all their killed in battle, the friends they found,
they bore at once into a common grave.
Now bishops and abbots in great number,   2955
monks, canons, tonsured priests stand in our ranks:
they absolved them, and blessed them in God's name,
and set burning myrrh and thymiama,
and censed their dead, in Rencesvals, with great ardor,
and buried them, when they were blessed, in great honor,   2960
and left them then: what more could they do there? AOI.

213.

The Emperor commands: prepare Roland,
and Oliver, and Archbishop Turpin;
has their bodies opened in his presence,
the hearts received in cloths of silk brocade,   2965
and laid in a coffin of white marble.
Then they took the remains of these good men,
and they wrapped the three lords in deerskin shrouds,
their bodies washed in spiced and fragrant wine.
The King commands Tedbalt and Gebuïn,   2970
Milun the Count, and Otun the Marquis:
"Escort these dead in three carts on their journey";
spread over them rich cloths of Eastern silk. AOI.

_____

214.

Charlemagne the Emperor wants to ride on
when before him the pagan vanguards rise.   2975
From their front ranks two messengers rode up;
they declare battle in the Amiral's name:
"No chance of running now, proud, puffed-up king!
See Baligant, he's riding after you,
and the great armies he leads from Araby!   2980
We'll see today what man there is in you." AOI.
And Charles the King grasped his white beard with that,
and remembers: the pain, all that he has lost;
looks with fierce pride on all his fighting men;
then he cries out, in his great, ringing voice: 2985
"Barons of France, brave men, to horse, to arms!" AOI.

215.

The Emperor is first to take up arms;
has put on with swift grace his coat of mail,
laces his helmet, has girded on Joiuse,
that sword of light the sun cannot obscure;   2990
hangs on his neck a shield of Gerona,
takes up his lance, lets the iron point swing;
then he mounts Tencendur, his good war horse—
he won that horse in the fords below Marsune,
threw Malpalin of Narbonne from the saddle dead—   2995
loosens the rein, spurs hard, gallops bounding
before the eyes of a hundred thousand men, AOI.
invokes the name of God and Rome's Apostle.

216.

Through all the field the men of France dismount,
all arm together, more than a hundred thousand;   3000
their battle gear is much to their liking,
their good, swift-running horses, their handsome arms;
now they are mounted: these men know how to ride!
let their time come, they mean to ride in battle:
the gonfalons flutter down to their helms.   3005
And when Charles sees the fair fighting look of them,
he calls aloud to Jozeran of Provence,
Naimon the Duke, and Antelme of Maience:
"These are vassals! men you can have faith in!
Only a fool would lose heart in their ranks.   3010
If the Arabs don't shrink back, if they come on,
I'll sell them dear, I swear, the death of Roland."
Naimon replies: "Now may God grant us that." AOI.

217.

King Charles summons Rabel and Guineman.
And the King said: "Seigneurs, I command you: 3015
Lords, take the places of Oliver and Roland:
you bear the sword, and you the olifant,
and both of you ride at the very head,
and fifteen thousand Franks in front with you,
the aspirants, the youth of our best men.   3020
And after them will come as many more;
these will be led by Gibuïns and Lorant."
Naimon the Duke and Jozeran the Count
put these divisions into good combat order.
Let their time come, there will be a great battle. AOI.   3025

2998. **Rome's Apostle:** Saint Peter, or his successor, the Pope.

3017. The sword of Oliver, the ivory horn of Roland. On the fate of Durendal, see
Menéndez Pidal, *La Chanson de Roland et la tradition épique*, pp. 174ff.

218.

The first divisions contain the men of France.
When these two have been set, they form the third:
in this one stand the vassals of Bavaria;
they were appraised at twenty thousand knights:
there'll be no flight from battle on their side.   3030
Under heaven there are no men whom Charles loves more,
except the men of France, who won the kingdoms.
Count Oger the Dane, that master warrior,
will lead this troop so furious for battle. AOI.

219.

The Emperor has three divisions now.   3035
Naimon the Duke orders into the fourth
certain barons, brave and faithful warriors,
the Alemanni, who come from Germany;
twenty thousand, as all the others reckon,
and well equipped, with good horses and arms: 3040
they'll never run, scared of dying, from battle.
Herman will lead these men, the Duke of Thrace
and never yet a coward: he would die first. AOI.

220.

Naimon the Duke and Jozeran the Count
formed the fifth corps, made it the Norman corps: 3045
they number twenty thousand, say all the Franks,
with handsome arms and fine swift-running horses;
they're not the sort who'll think things over again
        and then decide to yield: they would die first,
no abler men on the field under heaven!
Richard the Old will lead them into battle   3050
and strike where he leads them with his sharp spear. AOI.

221.

They formed the sixth division of Breton knights,
and thirty thousand men are mounted there,
and ride, each man the image of a knight,
their lances straight, their gonfalons affixed.   3055
The lord of the Bretons is named Eudon;
gives this command to Nevelun the Count,
Tedbald of Reims and Otun the Marquis:
"Here is my gift to you: lead my men." AOI.

222.

The Emperor has six divisions now.   3060
Naimon the Duke then formed the seventh corps
of Poitevins and barons of Auvergne:
here there might be some forty thousand men;
they stand with their good horses and handsome arms
apart, in a valley, beneath a hill,   3065
under the right hand of Charles, who blesses them.
Jozeran and Godselme will lead these men. AOI.

223.

Naimon the Duke has established the Eighth:
a corps of Flemings and barons of Friesland,
more than forty thousand good men in arms: 3070
there'll be no flight from battle in their ranks.
And the King said: "These men will serve me well."
Rembalt and Hamon of Galicia, in joint command,
will lead these men like brave lords into battle. AOI.

224.

And then Naimon and Jozeran the Count   3075
ordered good men into the ninth division:
they were men of Lorraine and Burgundy,
fifty thousand on horse, as they were counted,
armed in their mailed tunics, their helmets laced,
and strong spears in their hands: the wood is short.   3080
If the Arabs do not put off their coming,
if they attack, the Ninth will go at them
led by Tierri, the Duke of the Argonne. AOI.

225.

And now the Tenth: the veteran lords of France,
a hundred thousand of our greatest captain vassals—   3085
their bounding warriors' bodies and their proud look,
heads flowery white, and white their flowing beards,
hauberks drawn on, tunics of double mail;
they have put on their swords of France and Spain,
their fair shields bearing the emblems of their names—   3090
now they are mounted, and they demand the battle:
Munjoie! they shout, Charlemagne is with them!
Gefrei d'Anjou carries the Oriflamme:
it was Saint Peter's once, and called Romaine,
but in that battle it got the name Munjoie. AOI.   3095

3093–95. **The Oriflamme**: the banner of Charlemagne. The fact that it is the *vexillum Sancti Petri*, the flag of Saint Peter, identifies this battle as a holy war. See Carl Erdmann, *Die Entstehung des Kreuzzugsgedankens* (Stuttgart, 1935; reprinted Darmstadt, 1972), p. 178. Compare *laisses* 235, 242, and others.

226.

The Emperor now gets down from his horse;
on the green grass he lay face down to earth,
and turns his gaze towards the rising sun,
calls from the depths of his heart the name of God:
"You, true Father, stand with me on this day,   3100
You who saved Jonah, who brought him out in faith
from the great whale that had him in its body,
and You who spared the King of Nineveh,
and spared Daniel from suffering and dread
deep in the lions' den where he was cast,   3105
and the three children cast in the burning fire,
now, on this day, may Your love be with me:
and by Your grace, Lord, if it is Your will,
give me the strength to avenge my nephew, Roland."
When he has prayed, he rises to his feet;   3110
he signed his head with the power of the Cross.
And Charles the King mounts his swift-running horse—
Naimon and Jozeran held the stirrup—
takes up his shield, takes up his pointed lance:
his lordly body, well seated, breathing strength,   3115
his face aglow, the high-born king's look of him!
And then he rides, firmly horsed, unshakable.
The trumpets sound, to the rear, to the front:
the olifant's voice leaps beyond all the others;
and the French weep with all they feel for Roland.   3120

227.

The Emperor rides, the image of a lord.
He spread his beard outside upon his hauberk;
for love of him the others did the same:
a hundred thousand Franks, the veteran lords
of the Tenth Division, known now by this sign!
They come over these hills, these soaring cliffs,   3125
through these deep valleys, and, with much pain, they come
through these narrow defiles; come through these passes,
and through the wilderness, and then they entered
the Spanish march and camped on level ground.
The pagan scouts return to Baligant,   3130
a Syrian delivered this message:
"We have seen him, this Charlemagne, a proud king!
His men are fighters, they've no mind to desert him.
Take up your arms, you will soon have a battle."
Said Baligant: "These are words for brave men.   3135
Sound your trumpets so that my pagans know."

228.

Throughout the pagan host they sound their drums
and these trumpets and these high-pitched clarions,
and the pagans dismount to arm themselves.
The Amiral has no wish to delay,   3140
puts on his hauberk, the edges sewn with brass,
laces his helm, beset with gems in gold;
and then his sword: girds it on his left side;
in his presumption he found a name for it,
after Charles' sword, whose name he'd heard men speak: 3145
he gave his sword the name of Preciuse,
and on the field Preciuse! will be his cry:
he makes his warriors shout that sword's grand name.
Upon his neck he hangs a great broad shield,
the boss of gold, the border all of crystal,   3150
the strap brocaded silk adorned with rings;
takes up his lance—that lance he calls Maltét,
the shaft as thick around as a rafter,
the iron alone all that a mule could bear.
Now Baligant mounted his battle horse,   3155
Marcule from over sea held the stirrup.
What a great man! the fork of his legs immense,
the hips narrow, and the ribs broad and large,
the chest on him big and muscled like a lord's,
the shoulders wide, and his face full of light,   3160
the fierce look on him, his head covered with curls,
that grand white head, white as the summer flower.
How many times has his courage been tested!
God! he would have been great, had he been Christian!
He spurs his horse and its bright blood springs forth,   3165
gives it its head, leaps high over a ditch,
you can measure fifty feet across there.
The pagans shout: "Defender of the marches!
What man of France could come against our Lord
and have a choice—what could he do but die?   3170
Charlemagne is mad, he does not run away." AOI.

229.

The Admiral: the figure of a lord!
the beard on him is as white as a flower;
a wise and learned man in his religion,
and a savage in battle, a man of fury.   3175
And Malpramis, his son, a brave man mounted,
big and powerful, the image of his forebears;
said to his father: "Lord, let us ride out now.
I wonder though, shall we ever see Charles?"
Said Baligant: "Oh yes, Charles is very brave,   3180
chronicles praise him, songs are sung in his honor.
But he has no Roland, no nephew now,
he will not have the strength to withstand us." AOI.

230.

"Malpramis, my own son," said Baligant,
"Roland was killed yesterday, a great vassal,   3185
and Oliver, a good man, a brave man,
and the Twelve Peers, whom Charles so dearly loved,
and twenty thousand men with them, from France.
As for the others—not worth a glove, the whole lot.
The Emperor is coming back, that's certain,   3190
I've heard from my messenger, the Syrian,
who also said they have ten large divisions.
Hear the olifant now: a brave man there—
that high-pitched horn is his companion answering:
the two of them are riding at the head,   3195
and fifteen thousand Franks along with them,
the youngest ones, the ones Charles calls his children.
And after them there are as many more;
they will fight here with that wild pride of theirs."
Said Malpramis: "Let me have the first blow." AOI.   3200

231.

Said Baligant: "Malpramis, my dear son,
I grant you everything you've asked of me.
You'll leave at once to fight against the French,
and take Torleu, the Persian king, with you,
and Dapamort, a king too, of Leutice.   3205
If you can kill that savage pride of theirs,
I will give you a good strip of my land,
everything from Cheriant to Val Marchis."
And he replies: "Thank you, Lord! Thank you, Lord!"
He comes forward; and he received the gift—   3210
the land that had belonged to King Flurit—
in a bad hour, for he never saw it,
was never vested, he never got the land.

232.

The Amiral rides through the pagan host,
his son follows, a great big-bodied man.   3215
King Dapamort and King Torleu together
quickly make up thirty great battle corps,
they have men mounted in amazing force and numbers—
fifty thousand in the smallest division.
The first contains the men of Butentrot,   3220
the next Micenes, men with enormous heads:
over their backs, down the length of their spines,
they are covered with thick bristles like pigs. AOI.
And the third corps consists of Nubles and Blos,
and the fourth corps of the Bruns and the Slavs,   3225
and the fifth corps of the Slavonic Sorbs,
and the sixth corps of Armenians and Moors,
and the seventh of men from Jericho;
and the eighth corps of Nigres, the ninth of Gros,
and the tenth corps comes from Balide-la-Forte—   3230
there is a tribe that never wanted good! AOI.
The Emir swears, with every oath he knows,
by the body and the powers of Mahum:
"King Charles of France is riding here, a madman!
There'll be a battle if he does not withdraw—   3235
and no gold crown on his head any more."

233.

Then they make up another ten divisions:
the first of Canaanites, most ugly men—
they have come here by crossing Val-Fuït;
and the second of Turks, the third of Persians,   3240
and the fourth corps contains the Pinceneis;
formed the fifth corps of Soltras and Avars,
the sixth of Ormaleus and the Eugés,
the seventh of the men of Samuel;
the eighth corps is of Bruise, the ninth Clavers,   3245
the tenth of Occian, a desert land—
and there's a race that does not serve the Lord,
a pack of traitors, you'll never hear of worse,
the hides on those scoundrels as hard as iron,
and so they sneer at our helmets and hauberks;   3250
treacherous men in battle, and always coming on. AOI.

234.
The Amiral forms ten divisions more:
the first contains the giants of Malprose,
the second Huns, the third Hungarians;
and the fourth corps comes from Baldise-la-Lunge,   3255
the men of the fifth corps from Val Penuse,
and the men of the sixth . . . from Maruse;
Leus and Astrymonians in the seventh,
the eighth comes from Argoilles, the ninth Clarbone,
and in the tenth the longbears of Val Fronde—   3260
and there's a race that never did love God.
Thirty legions numbered in the Gesta Francorum,
immense armies where these trumpets resound:
the pagans ride, the image of good men. AOI.

235.
The Amiral is a great and mighty man.   3265
He orders his Dragon brought before him,
the banners of Mahum and Tervagant,
and an idol of Apolin, the betrayer.
And riding round about ten Canaanites
preach this sermon, their voices ringing loud: 3270
"Who seeks our gods' protection? Let him come forth
and pray, and serve, in deep humility."
And the pagans bow down their heads and chins,
and bend their fiery helms before their gods.
"You swine, you're all dead men!" the French cry out,   3275
"May this day see you broken and put to shame!
Lord of us all, protect King Charlemagne!
Let this battle be sworn in the name of the Lord." AOI.

236.
The Amiral is a man who knows war;
calls before him his son and the two kings: 3280
"Barons, my lords, you will ride at the head,
and show the way to all my battle corps;
but three of the best ones I want with me:
the Turkish corps, and then the Ormaleus,
and, third of all, the giants of Malprose.   3285
I'll keep with me the men of Occiant:
they'll take on Charles and his French tenth division.
If he stands and fights me, the Emperor
can count on losing the head on his shoulders,
that's the one right he'll have, he may be sure." AOI.   3290

3280. **The two kings:** Torleu, Dapamort (see *laisse* 231).

237.

These grand armies, these handsome battle corps!
No mountain stands between, no hill, no valley,
no woods, no forest: there is no place to hide;
they see each other clearly on that flat plain.
Said Baligant: "My own true heathen people,   3295
ride forward now, go and provoke the battle!
Amborre of Oluferne: you bear the ensign!"
The pagans shout, they cry that name: Preciuse!
And the French say: "You are lost men today!"
Munjoie! they shout, once more, with all their force.   3300
The Emperor commands them sound their horns,
that olifant! it sets their hearts on fire!
Say the pagans: "Charles' men look very good.
We'll have a battle, and it will be hard, and last long." AOI.

238.

It is a broad plain, the country round is wide,   3305
these helmets shine bedecked with gems in gold,
and all these shields, these hauberks edged with brass,
these spears, and fixed on them, these gonfanons;
these high-pitched trumpets sound, their voices clear,
that olifant, thundering the pursuit!   3310
And here the Amiral calls his brother,
Canabeus, the king of Floredée,
who held the land as far as Val Sevrée;
and he showed him the columns of Charles' army:
"That is the pride of France, the land they praise,   3315
the Emperor rides with a fury—look at his spirit!
he's in the rear, there! with those bearded troops:
they have spread their beards out over their hauberks,
see those white beards! like snow when the ground is frozen.
Those men will fight, they'll use their swords, their lances. 3320
We'll have a battle, it will be long and bitter,
no man has seen the fighting we shall see."
And further than one casts a branch stripped bare
Baligant rode ahead of his companions,
and spoke these words, these are the words he spoke: 3325
"Follow, Pagans, and I shall lead the way";
and with these words shook the handle of his spear
and turned the iron point toward Charlemagne. AOI.

239.

King Charles the Great, when he saw the Amiral,
and the Dragon, the standard, the gonfanon,   3330
the men of Araby in such great force
they covered every inch of that terrain
except the ground that the Emperor holds—
the King of France, seeing this, loudly calls:
"Barons of France, you are all my good vassals,   3335
the battles, Lords, in open fields you've fought!
There are the pagans, traitors and cowards all,
what's their whole religion worth to them now? not a penny!
and their swollen numbers—Lords, who cares about that?
Who will not ride with me? Let him depart!"—   3340
and digs his spurs into his warhorse then,
his Tencendor, who leaped for him four times.
And the French cry: "There is a warrior king!
Ride, noble lord, no man here will fail you."

240.

The day was clear, the sun was shining bright,   3345
and these hosts a fair sight, these batallions vast;
the forward ranks are at each other now.
Count Guineman and Count Rabel, in front,
loosen the reins to their swift-running horses,
dig in their spurs, the Franks charge at a gallop,   3350
and on they come to strike with their sharp spears. AOI.

241.

Rabel the Count: once mounted always charges,
digs with spurs of fine gold into his horse,
comes on to strike Torleu, the Persian king:
shield and hauberk could not withstand that blow;   3355
and drove into his body that gilded lance,
and threw him down on a little bush dead.
And the French say: "The Lord God be with us!
The right is with Charles, and we must not fail him." AOI.

242.

And Guineman charges a king of Leutice,   3360
smashes the shield painted so fair with flowers,
and then he tore the leather sewn with rings,
drove into him the whole length of his banner,
and cast him dead, now laugh or weep who will.
And with this blow the men of France cry out: 3365
"Barons, strike hard, brave men, do not hold back,
the right stands with King Charles against the pagans!
God has chosen us to reveal His true judgment." AOI.

243.

Malpramis sits upon a pure-white horse,
he hurls himself into the horde of French,   3370
and strikes great blows, and strikes again, and strikes,
time and again, casting dead upon dead.
And Baligant cries out, the first to speak:
"Lords of my house, the years I've nurtured you!
Look at my son, he is searching for Charles,   3375
how many barons he takes on with his arms!
How could I ever want a better vassal!
Stand by him now, help him, use your sharp spears!"
And with that word the pagans charge ahead,
and they strike hard: the fighting, the great slaughter,   3380
it is fearful, crushing—never, never
a battle so great, before or since that time. AOI.

244.

The vast armies, the furious batallions,
all these legions are at each other now,
and the pagans, how enormously they strike!   3385
God! how many spear shafts sundered, broken in two,
the shields in pieces, the hauberks' meshes shattered!
You would have seen, that day, the earth bestrewn,
and in the field the grass so green, so tender,
vermilion now with the blood shed there.   3390
The Amiral calls on the men he fostered:
"Strike, my brave lords, attack this Christian rabble!"
It is fearful, a battle to the end,
never before, such fighting, never since,
there'll be no end to it till death and night. AOI.   3395

245.

The Amiral calls out to all his people:
"Pagan men, fight! Strike, as you came to strike!
I will give you beautiful well-born women,
I will give you fiefs and honors and lands."
The pagans answer: "We are bound to fight well."   3400
And they strike hard, they break their lances striking,
and then they drew a hundred thousand swords, and more;
and here is fighting! here is terrible pain.
Who will stand in their midst? He'll see a battle! AOI.

3395. The fourth word of the line is missing in the manuscript. Some editors provide
nuit, others *mort*. The translation adopts both.

246.

The Emperor calls on his men of France: 3405
"Lords, I love you, I put my faith in you.
All the battles that you have fought for me,
all the kingdoms conquered, kings overthrown!
I declare it, I owe you gifts in return,
gifts of my person, gifts of land and treasure.   3410
Avenge your sons, your brothers, and your heirs,
avenge your dead who fell last night at Rencesvals!
For you know this: right is mine against the pagans."
The Franks reply: "Lord, it is the truth you speak."
He has with him some twenty thousand men,   3415
and with one voice they pledge their loyalty:
they'll not leave him though they suffer and die.
Every man strikes and uses up his lance,
and then at once they draw their swords and strike.
It is fearful, this huge and crushing battle. AOI.   3420

247.

Lord Malpramis comes riding through the field
and strikes great losses among the men of France.
Naimon the Duke measures him—with what fury!
comes on, good and valorous man, to strike,
breaks through the point and high edge of his shield,   3425
tears out the brass-sewn panels of his hauberk,
thrusts into him the yellow length of his banner,
throws him down, dead, with seven hundred others.

248.

King Canabeus, the Amiral's own brother,
drives in his spurs, digs hard into his horse;   3430
he has drawn out his crystal-handed sword,
strikes, on that prince's helm, Naimon the Duke,
shatters the half of it, all on one side,
cuts through five laces with the steel of his sword,
the hood of mail not worth one cent to Naimon;   3435
cuts through the coif into the very flesh,
knocks to the ground a piece of Naimon's flesh—
a mighty blow, Naimon was thunderstruck,
and would have fallen, but for the hand of God.
He got his arms round the neck of his horse.   3440
Now had the pagan come at hime one more time,
that great vassal would have been a dead man.
Charles of France came to him. He will be saved. AOI.

249.

Naimon the Duke is held fast in great distress;
Charles must strike quickly, the pagan presses him.   3445
Said Charles: "You serf! You died when you struck him!"—
and falls on him—the courage of that king!—
smashes his shield, shatters it on his heart,
tears to pieces the hauberk's hood of mail,
throws him down, dead, there sits the saddle empty.   3450

250.

Charlemagne the King is filled with pain and rage
when he sees before him Duke Naimon wounded,
and on the green grass that bright and famous blood;
and gave him this soft word of good counsel:
"Naimon, dear lord, now come and ride with me,   3455
the swine is dead who had you in distress,
I drove my lance one good time through his body."
The Duke replies: "Lord, I put my faith in you;
if I should live, the good in me is yours";
rode side by side, in love and loyalty,   3460
and there with them, some twenty thousand French,
there is not one who does not thrust and strike. AOI.

251.

The Amiral rides through the battlefield,
and now comes on to strike Count Guineman,
shatters the shield all white against his heart,   3465
and tears to shreds the panels of his hauberk,
cuts the rib cage away from side to side,
throws him down, dead, from his swift-running horse.
And then he killed: Gebuïn and Lorant,
Richard the Old, the lord of the Normans.   3470
The pagans shout: "Preciuse! that priceless sword!
Brave Barons, strike! there rides our defender." AOI.

252.

Oh to have seen the knights of Araby,
those men of Occiant, Argoille, and Bascle!
the blows they strike, the thrusting of their lances!   3475
The men of France—they have no wish to run.
Many men die, on this side, on that side.
All through the day till evening the fighting is hard,
among the Franks, brave men, there are great losses.
There will be grief before the battle ends. AOI.   3480

253.

The men of France and Araby strike hard,
these wooden shafts, these burnished lances shatter.
Whoever then had seen these shields in pieces,
heard the ringing of hauberks shining white,
the grating of these swords upon these helms;   3485
whoever then had seen these warriors falling,
and men roaring and dying on the ground,
would always keep the memory of pain.
It is a battle, and very hard to bear.
The Amiral calls the name of Apollin,   3490
the names of Tervagant and Mahumet:
"My lords, my gods, I have served you long and well.
I shall make your idols of purest gold: AOI.
only protect me now from Charlemagne."
Now Gemalfin, one of his dearest men,   3495
is standing before him, and with bad news:
"Baligant, Lord, it goes against you today.
Your Malpramis—you have lost him, your son,
and Canabeus, your brother, has been killed—
it was two men of France, they had great luck,   3500
the emperor, I'm sure, was one of them:
big in body, with the look of a lord,
the beard on him white as an April flower."
The Amiral's helmet bows down with that,
and then, with that, he looks down to the earth;   3505
and feels such pain, he thought at once of dying;
and called to him Jangleu, from beyond the sea.

254.

The Emir spoke: "Jangleu, come forward now,
you are a good man and your knowledge is great,
and your counsel has always guided me.   3510
How does it look between Arabs and Franks?
Will our side win, is the battlefield ours?"
This man replies: "You are dead, Baligant!
Those gods of yours will never protect you.
Charles comes in fury, the men with him are brave—   3515
I have never seen men so full of war.
But now call out the barons of Occiant,
Turks and Enfruns, the Arabs, the Giants.
Do not delay whatever has to be."

255.

The Amiral spread his beard on his hauberk,   3520
white as the flower on the hawthorn branch;
whatever comes, this man will never hide;
sets to his lips a high- bright-sounding trumpet,
sounds its clear voice, and all the pagans heard,
through all the field they rally their companions;   3525
the men of Occiant whinny and bray,
and the men of Argoille, they bark like dogs;
and fall upon the French with such blind rage,
they broke apart and split their thickest ranks,
struck with this blow seven thousand men dead.   3530

256.

Count Oger never learned to be a coward,
no better man ever wore the hauberk;
and when he saw the French ranks break apart,
he called Tierri, the Duke of the Argonne,
Gefrei d'Anjou, and Jozeran the Count;   3535
and speaks these words, fiercely, proudly, to Charles:
"See the pagans, see them killing your men!
May the Crown on your head offend the Lord
unless you strike at once to avenge your shame!"
And no man there says one word in reply: 3540
they all spur hard, they let their horses run,
they'll strike the foe wherever they may find him.

257.

King Charlemagne strikes hard in that assault, AOI.
Naimon the Duke, Oger the Dane, they strike,
Gefrei d'Anjou, the standard-bearer, strikes.   3545
What a brave man, my lord Oger the Dane!
he spurs his horse, lets it run, the reins loose,
comes on to strike the man who held the Dragon,
and brings Ambure crashing down to the earth,
and the Dragon, and the ensign of the King.   3550
Baligant sees: his gonfanon brought down,
and Mahumet's banner grounded in grief:
the Amiral begins to see, somewhat,
that he is wrong, that Charlemagne is right.
Silence comes over the pagans of Araby.   3555
The Emperor calls to his men of France:
"Tell me, Barons, by God, will you help me?"
The Franks reply: "That you should ask us that!
Who will not fight with joy? Call him a traitor!" AOI.

3546. Many editors believe that this line should be omitted and the following attack
attributed to Gefrei d'Anjou, as in the other versions; then it is a battle between the
two standard-bearers.

258.

The day goes by and passes into evening,   3560
and on that field Franks and pagans strike with swords.
They are brave men who led these hosts to battle,
nor did they once forget their battle cries—
Preciuse! Preciuse! the Amiral cried out,
and Charles, Munjoie! that great and famous word—   3565
and knew each other by their great ringing voices.
And now they met in the midst of the field,
and they fall to—what are the blows they strike
with their great lances on shields adorned with rings,
the spear shafts break, shattered on these wide bosses;   3570
they tore away the panels of their hauberks,
but never touched the body intact within;
the saddlegirths are broken, down came the saddles,
and down they fall: two Kings are on the ground,
and on their feet—with what swift grace!—once more,   3575
drew out their swords, fierce and valorous old men.
Nothing can turn aside this battle now,
it cannot end without one of them dead. AOI.

259.

Charles of sweet France: a mighty warrior!
The Emir does not fear him, he knows no fear.   3580
And on that field they raise their naked swords,
and then the blows they strike on these strong shields
slice through the leather, the double layers of wood,
the nails fly out, the wide bosses shatter;
and then, bare of shields now, strike on their hauberks,   3585
and sparks of fire leap from their blazing helms.
There'll be no end, this battle cannot stop
till one of them confesses he is wrong. AOI.

260.

Said the Emir: "Charles, it is time to take thought,
make up your mind: show me that you repent.   3590
You killed my son, I know that it was you,
and challenge me—a great wrong—for my own land.
Become my man, I'll give you the land as fief,
come and serve me from here to the Orient."
And Charles replies: "How vile that sounds to me!   3595
That I should grant a pagan peace or love!
Receive the law that God holds out to us,
the Christian faith: I'll love you from that moment;
believe in Him, serve the Almighty King!"
Said Baligant: "You preach a bad sermon."   3600
And then they strike with the swords at their sides. AOI.

261.

The Amiral is a man of great strength;
strikes Charlemagne on his helm of bright steel,
and he broke it, cleaved it upon his head;
drives the sword into the fine thick hair, 3605
takes from his flesh a hand's breadth, and more;
where that blow struck, the bone is left all bare.
Charles staggers, would have fallen—comes very close;
but God does not want him to die or fall.
Saint Gabriel has come back by his side, 3610
and he demands: "Great King, what are you doing?"

262.

When King Charles hears the angel's holy voice,
he has no fear, he has no dread of death,
strength and memory come home to him again;
and he strikes the Emir with the sword of France, 3615
shatters his helm, where the gems cast their fires,
cuts through the head, the brain comes pouring out,
and through the face, down to the great white beard,
throws him down, dead, he will not rise again.
Munjoie! he shouts, for a sign to his men. 3620
And with this word there came Naimon the Duke,
and he holds Tencendur: the great King mounts.
The pagans turn, they do not stand, they flee:
it is God's will; and now the men of France
  are on the heels of all that they desire.

263.

The pagans flee: it is as the Lord wills; 3625
the French pursue, the Emperor with them;
and the King said: "Seigneurs, avenge your griefs,
strike and bring peace to your hearts and desires—
for this morning I saw your eyes weeping."
The Franks reply: "That is our duty, Lord"; 3630
and they strike hard, each strikes with all his might.
Of the pagans, few who were there that day escaped.

264.

The heat that day is great, dust rises up,
the pagans flee, the French do not let them breathe;
the chase goes on from here to Saragossa.　3635
Bramimunde climbed to the top of her tower,
and with her there her priests and her canons
of that false religion, a bad faith God never loved:
they have no orders, no tonsures on their heads.
And when she saw the Arabs shamed and beaten,　3640
she cried aloud: "Mahumet, help us all!
Oh! noble King, look at that, our men defeated,
and the Amiral killed, and in such shame!"
And Marsilion, hearing that, turns to the wall,
tears fill his eyes, he weeps, he bows his head,　3645
is dead of grief, weighed down by sin and calamity.
He gives his soul to the living devils. AOI.

265.

Pagans are dead, a few have turned to flight,
and Charlemagne the King has won his battle.
He has knocked down the gate of Saragossa,　3650
he knows well now: it will not be defended;
takes the city, his army entered in,
and there they lay that night: the power is theirs.
Proud and fierce is this King whose beard is white.
Bramimunde gave the towers into his hands,　3655
the ten great towers, the fifty smaller towers.
A man fares well when the Lord is with him.

266.

The day wears on, the night has gathered now,
the moon shines bright, the stars are all ablaze,
the Emperor has taken Saragossa.　3660
He sends a thousand French to search the city,
the synagogues, the mosques of Mahumet,
with iron mauls and hatchets in their hands,
they break the images, shatter all idols:
there shall be no more magic and no more fraud.　3665
The King believes in God, he has one will:
to serve the Lord; and his bishops bless the waters,
lead the pagans to the baptismal font:
if there is one who now refuses Charles,
he has that man struck dead, or hanged, or burned;　3670
and they baptized more than a hundred thousand
true Christians all, but not Queen Bramimunde:
she will be led, a captive, to sweet France:
the King wants her led to conversion by love.

267.

Night passes on, and the bright day appears.   3675
Charles fortified the towers of Saragossa,
left a thousand knights there, fighting men all;
they guard the city in the Emperor's name.
Now the King mounts his horse, all his men mount,
and Bramimunde, whom he leads prisoner,   3680
though he has but one will: to do her good.
They turn toward home, in joy, in jubilation,
and pass in force, a mighty host, through Nerbone;
and Charles came to Bordeaux, that . . . city, sets
on the altar of the baron saint Sevrin   3685
the olifant, filled with gold and pagan coins—
pilgrims passing can see it there today;
crosses the Gironde in great ships that lie there;
he has escorted as far as Blaye his nephew
and Oliver, his noble companion,   3690
and the Archbishop, who was so wise and brave;
and bids these lords be laid in white stone coffins:
at Saint-Romain the brave men lie there still;
the Franks leave them to the Lord and His Names.
And Charles rides over the valleys and the mountains,   3695
would take no rest all the long way to Aix,
and rode until he dismounts at the steps.
When he is in his sovereign high palace,
he summons all his judges, sends messengers:
Saxons, Bavarians, Frisians, men of Lorraine,   3700
the Alemans, the men of Burgundy,
the Poitevins, the Normans, the Bretons,
the wisest men among the men of France.
And now begins the trial of Ganelon.

Laisse 267. The action interrupted at line 2973 now resumes.

3684. The line is incomplete in the manuscript.

3694. **The Lord and His Names:** a reference to prayers containing some of the many names (Adonai, Emmanuel, Yehovah, and so on) by which God is called in sacred writings. These prayers were considered effective in times of danger.

268.

The Emperor is home again from Spain,   3705
and comes to Aix, best residence of France,
ascends to the palace; entered the hall.
And now comes Aude, fair maid, before the King;
and said to him: "Where is Roland the captain,
who swore to me to take me for his wife?"   3710
And Charlemagne feels the weight and grief of this,
tears fill his eyes, he weeps, pulls his white beard:
"Sweet friend, dear sister, you ask for a dead man.
I will give you a good man in his place,
it is Louis, I cannot name a better—   3715
he is my son, he will possess my marches."
And Aude replies: "How strange these words sound to me.
May it never please God or his angels or saints
that I should go on living after Roland";
loses color, falls at Charlemagne's feet,   3720
already dead, God take pity on her soul.
Brave men of France weep and lament for Aude.

269.

Aude the fair maid is gone now to her end;
the King believes that she has only fainted;
and he is moved, the Emperor weeps for Aude,   3725
takes her two hands; now he has raised her up,
her head sinks down, fallen upon her shoulders;
when Charlemagne sees she is dead in his arms,
he has four countesses sent for at once,
and Aude is borne to a minster of nuns;   3730
all through the night till dawn they wake beside her,
then nobly buried her by an altar.
The King gave Aude great honors, the church great gifts. AOI.

270.

The Emperor has come home again to Aix.
In iron chains, the traitor Ganelon   3735
stands before the palace, within the city.
He has been bound, and by serfs, to a stake;
they tie his hands with deerhide straps and thongs,
and beat him hard, with butcher's hooks, with clubs—
for what better reward has this man earned?   3740
There he stands, in pain and rage, awaiting his trial.

271.

It is written in the ancient Geste
that Charles summons his vassals from many lands;
they are gathered in the chapel at Aix,
a high day this, a very solemn feast,   3745
the feast, some say, of the baron saint Sylvester.
Now here begin the trial and the pleadings
of Ganelon, who committed treason.
The Emperor has had this man brought forth. AOI.

272.

"Barons, my lords," said Charlemagne the King,   3750
"judge what is right concerning Ganelon.
He was with me, came in my army to Spain,
and took from me twenty thousand of my French,
and my nephew, whom you'll not see again,
and Oliver, brave man, born to the court,   3755
and the Twelve Peers—betrayed them all for money."
Said Ganelon: "Let me be called a traitor
        if I hide what I did. It was Roland
who cheated me of gold and goods; and so I wanted
to make him suffer and die; and found the way.
But treason, no—I'll grant no treason there!"   3760
The Franks reply: "We shall take counsel now."

273.

And there Ganelon stood, before the King,
breathing power—that lordly color on his face:
the image of a great man, had he been loyal.
He sees his judges, he sees the men of France,   3765
and his kinsmen, the thirty with him there;
then he cried out, with that great ringing voice:
"Barons, hear me, hear me for the love of God!
I was in that army with the Emperor
and served him well, in love and loyalty.   3770
Then his nephew Roland began to hate me,
and he doomed me to die an outrageous death:
I was sent as messenger to King Marsilion.
I used my wits, and I came back alive.
Now I had challenged Roland, that great fighter,   3775
and Oliver, and all of their companions:
King Charles heard it, and all his noble barons.
I took *revenge*, but there's no treason there."
The Franks reply: "We shall go into council."

3746. The feast of Saint Sylvester: December 31.

274.

When Ganelon sees that his great trail commences,   3780
he got his thirty kinsmen all around him.
There is one man the others listen to:
it is Pinabel of the castle of Sorence,
a man who counsels well and judges well,
a valiant fighter—no man can win his arms. AOI.   3785
Said Ganelon: "In you, friend . . .
free me from death and from this accusation!"
Said Pinabel: "You will soon be out of this.
Let one Frenchman dare sentence you to hang:
once the Emperor sets us down man to man,   3790
I will give him the lie with this steel sword."
And Ganelon, the Count, falls at his feet.

275.

Bavarians, Saxons have gone into council,
Poitevins and Normans and men of France,
the Alemans, the Germans from the North,   3795
men of Auvergne, the courtliest of all.
They keep their voices low, because of Pinabel;
said to each other: "Best to let it stop here—
let's leave this trial and then entreat the King
to let Count Ganelon go free this time   3800
and serve henceforth in love and loyalty.
Roland is dead: you won't see him again,
he will not come for gold or goods again:
only a fool would fight over this now."
All go along, no one there disagrees   3805
except one man, Lord Gefrei's brother: Tierri. AOI.

276.

The barons now come back to Charlemagne,
say to the King: "Lord, this we beg of you:
let Ganelon go free, renounce your claim,
then let him serve you in love and loyalty: 3810
let this man live, for his family is great.
Roland is dead: we'll not see a hair of him,
        though we die for it, not a shred of his garment,
or get him back for gold or goods again."
And the King said: "You are all my traitors." AOI.

3786. The line is incomplete in the manuscript.

277.

When Charles perceives all have abandoned him,   3815
he bowed his head with that and hid his face,
and in such pain calls himself wretched man.
But now we see: a warrior before him,
Tierri, brother of Gefrei, a duke of Anjou—
the meager body on him, such a slight man!   3820
his hair all black, and his face rather dark;
hardly a giant, but at least not too small;
said to the Emperor, as one born to the court:
"Dear Lord and King, do not lament before us.
You know I have served you well: I have the right,   3825
my forebears' right! to give this judgment here:
Whatever wrong Count Roland may have done
to Ganelon, he was in your service,
        and serving you should have protected him.
Ganelon is a traitor: he betrayed Roland.
It's you he wronged when he perjured himself,   3830
and broke faith. Therefore, I sentence him
to die, to hang . . . his body cast . . .
like a traitor, a man who committed treason.
If his kinsman wants to give me the lie,
here is my sword, girded on: and with this sword   3835
I am ready to make my judgment good."
The Franks reply: "Now you have spoken well."

278.

Now Pinabel has come before the King:
a huge man of swift grace, a valiant man—
time has run out for the poor wretch he strikes!—   3840
said to the King: "Lord, is this not your court?
Give orders then, tell them to stop this noise.
Here I see Tierri, who has given his judgment:
I declare it is false; I shall fight with him";
places his deerhide glove in Charles's fist.   3845
Said the Emperor: "I must have good surety."
Thirty kinsmen go hostage for his loyalty.
Then the King said: "I shall release him then";
and has them guarded until justice is done. AOI.

3832. Line incomplete in manuscript.

279.

When Tierri sees the battle will take place   3850
he gave to Charles his own right glove as gage.
The Emperor sets him free, for hostages;
then has four benches set round that battle ground:
there they will sit: the two men pledged to fight.
The others judge they have been duly summoned,   3855
Oger of Denmark had settled every question.
And then they call for their horses and arms.

280.

Now since both men have been brought forth for battle, AOI.
they make confession and are absolved and blessed;
they hear their mass, receive the Sacrament,   3860
lay down great offerings in these minsters.
Now the two men have come back before Charles.
They have fastened their spurs upon their feet,
and they put on white hauberks, strong and light,
and laced their bright helmets glowing upon their heads,   3865
gird on their swords, the hilts of purest gold;
hang their great quartered shields upon their necks,
take hold of their sharp spears in their right fists;
now they are mounted upon their swift war horses.
And then a hundred thousand warriors wept,   3870
moved for love of Roland to pity Tierri.
The Lord well knows how this battle will end.

281.

Down below Aix there is a broad meadow;
there the battle is joined between these barons.
They are brave men, great warriors keeping faith,   3875
and their horses are swift and spirited.
They spur them hard, reins loosened all the way,
come on to strike, the great strength that is theirs!
their two shields burst in that attack to pieces,
their hauberks tear, their saddle girths rip open,   3880
the bosses turn, the saddles fall to earth.
A hundred thousand men, who watch them, weep.

Laisse 279. Pinabel and Tierri will now fight a judicial duel to get an answer from God to the question before the court: What is the nature of Ganelon's act—was it treason or revenge?

282.

Now the two warriors are on the ground, AOI.
now on their feet, and with what speed! again—
the grace and lightness, the strength of Pinabel!—   3885
fall on each other, they have no horses now,
strike with their swords, the hilts of purest gold,
and strike again on these helmets of steel
tremendous blows—blows that cut through helms of steel!   3890
The knights of France are wild with grief and worry.
"Oh, God," said Charles, "make the right between
        them clear!"

283.

Said Pinabel: "Tierri, now give it up!
I'll be your man, in love and loyalty,
I'll give you all I own, take what you please,
only make peace with the King for Ganelon."   3895
Tierri replies: "I cannot hear of that,
call me traitor if I consent to that!
May God do right between us two today." AOI.

284.

Now Tierri spoke: "Pinabel, you are good,
the great body on you formed like a lord's;   3900
your peers know you: all that a vassal should be;
let this battle go then, let it end here,
I will make peace for you with Charlemagne.
But justice will be done on Ganelon,
        such justice will be done on his body,
no day will pass that men do not speak of it."   3905
Said Pinabel: "May the Lord God forbid!
I will stand up for all my kin, I'll fight,
no man alive will make me quit my kin
        and cry defeat and beg for his mercy,
I'd sooner die than be reproached for that."
And they begin to beat down with their swords   3910
on these helmets beset with gems in gold,
and the bright fires fly from that fight toward heaven;
and no chance now that these two can be parted:
it cannot end without one of them dead. AOI.

285.

Pinabel of Sorence, that valiant man,   3915
strikes Tierri now on that helm of Provence:
the fire shoots out and sets the grass aflame;
and shows Tierri the point of that steel sword:
he brought it down. Pinabel brought it down
on his forehead, and down across his face,   3920
the whole right cheek is bloody from that blow,
his hauberk runs with blood down to his waist.
God protects him, he is not struck down dead. AOI.

286.

And Tierri sees: he is struck on the face—
the bright blood falling on the grass in the meadow;   3925
strikes Pinabel on his helm of bright steel,
and shattered it, split it to the nosepiece,
struck his brain out spattering from his head;
and raised his sword; he has cast him down, dead.
That was the blow, and the battle is won.   3930
The Franks cry out: "God has made a miracle!
Now Ganelon must hang, it is right now,
and all his kin who stood for him in court." AOI.

287.

Now when Tierri had won his great battle,
there came to him the Emperor Charlemagne,   3935
and forty of his barons along with him,
Naimon the Duke, and Oger of Denmark,
William of Blaye, and Gefrei of Anjou.
The King has taken Tierri into his arms,
he wipes his face with his great furs of marten,   3940
throws them aside; they clasp new furs round him.
Very gently, they disarm the warrior,
then they mount him on a mule of Araby,
and he comes home in joy among brave men.
They come to Aix, it is there they dismount.   3945
It is the time now for the executions.

288.

Now Charlemagne summons his counts and dukes:
"What is your counsel regarding those I have held?
They came to court to stand for Ganelon,
bound themselves hostages for Pinabel."   3950
The Franks reply: "Not one of them must live."
The King commands his officer, Basbrun:
"Go, hang them all on the accursed tree,
and by this beard, by the white hairs in this beard,
if one escapes, you are lost, a dead man."   3955
Basbrun replies: "What should I do but hang them?";
leads them, by force, with a hundred sergeants.
They are thirty men, and thirty men are hanged.
A traitor brings death, on himself and on others. AOI.

289.

Bavarians and Alemans returned,   3960
and Poitevins, and Bretons, and Normans,
and all agreed, the Franks before the others,
Ganelon must die, and in amazing pain.
Four war horses are led out and brought forward;
then they attach his two feet, his two hands.   3965
These battle horses are swift and spirited,
four sergeants come and drive them on ahead
toward a river in the midst of a field.
Ganelon is brought to terrible perdition,
all his mighty sinews are pulled to pieces,   3970
and the limbs of his body burst apart;
on the green grass flows that bright and famous blood.
Ganelon died a traitor's and recreant's death.
Now when one man betrays another,
       it is not right that he should live to boast of it.

290.

When the Emperor had taken his revenge,   3975
he called to him his bishops of France,
Bavaria, Germany: "In my household
there is a noble captive, and she has heard,
for so long now, such sermons and examples,
she longs for faith in God, the Christian faith.   3980
Baptize this Queen, that God may have her soul."
And they reply: "Let her be baptized now
by godmothers, ladies of noble birth."
At the baths of Aix there is a great crowd gathered,
there they baptized the noble Queen of Spain,   3985
and they found her the name Juliana;
she is Christian, by knowledge of the Truth.

291.

When the Emperor had brought his justice to pass
and peace comes now to that great wrath of his,
he put the Christian faith in Bramimunde;   3990
the day passes, the soft night has gathered,
the King lay down in his vaulted chamber.
Saint Gabriel! come in God's name to say:
"Charles, gather the great hosts of your Empire!
Go to the land of Bire, with all your force,   3995
you must relieve King Vivien at Imphe,
the citadel, pagans have besieged it:
Christians are calling you, they cry your name!"
The Emperor would have wished not to go.
"God!" said the King, "the pains, the labors of my life!";   4000
weeps from his eyes, pulls his white beard.

Here ends the song	that Turold composes, paraphrases, amplifies,	4002
	that Turold completes, relates,	
Here ends the tale	that Turold declaims, recounts, narrates,	
	that Turold copies, transcribes,	
Here ends the geste	for Turold grows weak, grows weary, declines,	
Here ends the written history,		
Here ends the source	that Turold turns into poetry.	

4002. The last line of the poem reads *Ci falt la geste que Turoldus declinet.* The meaning of the words *geste* and *declinet* and the syntax of *que* have never been finally settled, and no line in the poem contains so many possible meanings as the last one. Some of the interpretations that have been proposed are given here, and every one is plausible.